A Grief Received

A Grief Received

What to Do When Loss Leaves You Empty-Handed

JL Gerhardt

A GRIEF RECEIVED
What to Do When Loss Leaves You Empty-Handed

Cover design: Rob Dewey

Print ISBN: 978-1-5064-3176-5
eBook ISBN: 978-1-5064-3420-9

The paper used in this publication meets the minimum requirements of American National Standard for Information Sciences — Permanence of Paper for Printed Library Materials, ANSI Z329.48-1984.

Manufactured in the U.S.A.

Contents

Series Preface

MY MOST sincere wish is that the Living with Hope series will offer comfort, wisdom—and hope—to individuals facing life's most common and intimate challenges. Books in the series tackle complex problems such as addiction, parenting, unemployment, pregnancy loss, serious illness, trauma, and grief and encourage individuals, their families, and those who care for them. The series is bound together by a common message for those who are dealing with significant issues: you are not alone. There is hope.

This series offers first-person perspectives and insights from authors who know personally what it is like to face these struggles. As companions and guides, series contributors share personal experiences, offer valuable research from trusted experts, and suggest questions to help readers process their own responses and explore possible next steps. With empathy and honesty, these accessible volumes reassure individuals they are not alone in their pain, fear, or confusion.

The series is also a valuable resource for pastoral and spiritual care providers in faith-based settings. Parish pastors, lay ministers, chaplains, counselors, and other staff and volunteers can draw on these volumes to offer skilled and compassionate guidance to individuals in need of hope.

Each title in this series is offered with prayer for the reader's journey—one of discovery, further challenges, and transformation. You are not alone. There is hope.

Beth Ann Gaede, Series Editor

Titles in the Living with Hope Series

Nurturing Hope: Christian Pastoral Care in the Twenty-First Century (Lynne M. Baab)

Dignity and Grace: Wisdom for Caregivers and Those Living with Dementia (Janet L. Ramsey)

Jobs Lost, Faith Found: A Spiritual Resource for the Unemployed (Mary C. Lindberg)

They Don't Come with Instructions: Cries, Wisdom, and Hope for Parenting Children with Developmental Challenges (Hollie M. Holt-Woehl)

True Connection: Using the NAME IT Model to Heal Relationships (George Faller and Heather P. Wright)

Waiting for Good News: Living with Chronic and Serious Illness (Sally L. Wilke)

Carrying Them with Us: Living through Pregnancy or Infant Loss (David M. Engelstad and Catherine A. Malotky)

A Grief Received: What to Do When Loss Leaves You Empty-Handed (JL Gerhardt)

When Trauma Wounds: Pathways to Healing and Hope (Karen A. McClintock)

Addiction and Recovery: A Spiritual Pilgrimage (Martha Postlethwaite)

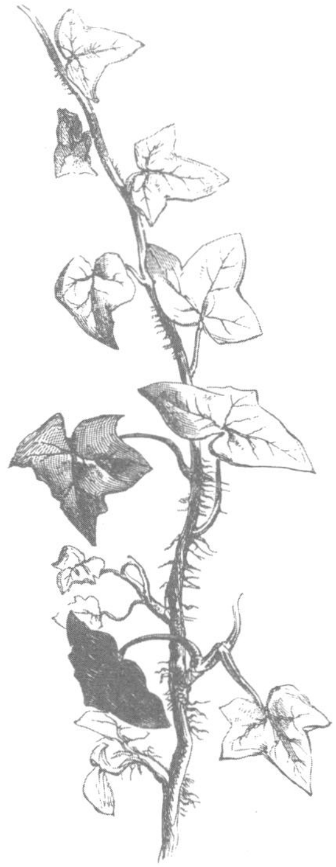

Acknowledgments

THIS BOOK benefits from the brave generosity of so many who shared their stories of loss with me and now with you. Some of their names have been changed, some haven't. All of them represent people I love and admire, people I'm rooting for as they endure and embrace grief.

Thank you, Beth Gaede, for so thoughtfully editing this book. You've been kind and helpful—the two virtues I most admire in a person.

Thank you, Bromleigh McCleneghan, for recommending me to Fortress Press, for opening doors to which I didn't have keys.

Thanks to everyone at the Collegeville Institute, particularly the writers who gathered to study and share under the direction of Tom Long in the summer of 2017. You helped make this book possible.

Thank you, Mom and Dad, for grieving with courage and perseverance. Your example has been inspiring.

Thank you, London and Eve. While finishing up this book I told you, "I may be the worst mom ever for the next few weeks." Your grace and your generous encouragement ("You're the best worst mom ever") made the work lighter.

Thank you, Justin, for grieving by my side with grace and wisdom. Thank you for saying such quotable things. Thank you for showing me how to cultivate joy.

Thank you, God, for opening my eyes to your work in my pain. Thank you for hope, comfort, transformation, for every gift you've given in grief.

1

Changing Shape

I was twenty-one when my brother died. The night before his early morning car crash, I hosted friends in my brand-new red-brick home. I served lasagna, played games, took pictures. Only one of those pictures survives, and when I look at it (I hardly ever look at it) I don't much recognize the woman I see staring back. In the 4×6 glossy, black-and-white print, my husband and I sit cross-legged in front of our very first Christmas tree. There's a fire in the fireplace to my right, stockings hung on the mantel. Though I am just twenty-one, I'm married and have a mortgage. In ten hours I'll be twenty-one, married, mortgaged, and mourning my twenty-year-old brother and best friend.

I don't like to look at this picture, to look at this young woman I hardly recognize, this woman who thinks she's safe. Her eyes sparkle, her smile wide and innocent. I want to protect her from what comes next, to at least warn her. But no siren passes from here to there. Tomorrow she will wake to an ambush.

In the picture I'm newly brunette, having dyed my hair this ill-fitting color on a whim. Sometimes I think this girl must be my dark-haired cousin, like me but not me. I look at the picture, the last one taken of me before my brother died, and it's like stepping through a portal into another dimension—Before.

On the morning after the moment in this picture my grandfather will call and tell me my brother didn't make it home, that his car's not in the driveway though it should be, that his body's not in his bed. My grandfather will ask me to pray. I will.

And then he'll call back, no more than two minutes after I've said amen. "Jennifer, Bobby's dead."

BECAUSE THIS is a book about grief, and because it's in your hands, I expect my story isn't foreign. You likely have your own early morning phone call story. Or maybe a late night by the hospital bed story. Perhaps you found out like my mother did, when a policeman arrived at your door, a policeman you couldn't bear to let in. Maybe a doctor put her hands in her wide, white pockets, her eyes on the floor as she walked toward you, and you knew before she said a word.

If you've had a moment like this, you'll never forget it. You'll remember the shirt you were wearing, the color of the paint in the hospital waiting room, the smell of Lysol wafting in from the hall, the exact tone of the ringing phone. For the rest of your life, it'll be the moment when everything changed, a permanent hash mark of time and identity. We, the grieving, catalogue our lives by our loss, everything Before or After, everything pre- or post-phone call, diagnosis, knock.

We, the grieving, catalogue our lives by our loss, everything Before or After, everything pre- or post-phone call, diagnosis, knock.

If you're living in the After, you know, it's different here.

After my brother died, people talked about things eventually getting back to "normal," said they'd give me time to "recover." I imagine they thought of my loss like a broken bone, something to set right. The idea was to leave the bone alone, protect it from bumps, and wait. Eventually everything would be back to normal, the same as it always was. *Time heals all wounds and whatnot.* Though suspicious, I pursued this course of action (inaction), and waited for normal, but normal never came. Looking back through the filter of experience and hard-won wisdom, I know why: Losing a loved one is nothing like breaking an arm. Losing a loved one is like *losing* an arm. Loss is medically unnecessary, criminally unauthorized amputation.

C. S. Lewis wrote in *A Grief Observed* about the loss of his wife and his subsequent grief:

> To say the patient is getting over it after an operation for appendicitis is one thing; after he's had his leg off is quite another. After that operation either the wounded stump heals or the man dies. If it heals, the fierce, continuous pain will stop. Presently he'll get back his strength and be able to stump about on his wooden leg. He has "got over it." But he will probably have recurrent pains in the stump all his life, and perhaps pretty bad ones; and he will always be a one-legged man. There will be hardly any moment when he forgets it. Bathing, dressing, sitting down and getting up again, even lying in bed, will all be different. . . . At present I am learning to get about on crutches. Perhaps I shall presently be given a wooden leg. But I shall never be a biped again.[1]

He will always be a one-legged man.

At my brother's funeral, dressed in a crisp black dress and pantyhose, my hair curled and piled neatly, I stood in front of five hundred people and tried to describe what it felt like to lose my brother. As the writer in the family, I was asked to share words, words I couldn't find. I look back at what I wrote and see myself struggling to muster a voice, struggling to know who I am in the shadow of loss. I said, groping for truth, "It feels like I've lost a limb."

Little bits of ourselves live in other people's minds.

Daniel Wegner in his research on what he calls transactive memory determined that we often store things in the minds of those we love and live with and work alongside. Malcolm Gladwell, reflecting on this phenomenon, said it's like "Little bits of ourselves [live] in other people's minds."[2] If that's true, when those people die, little bits of us (or heaps and piles and towers of little bits) die, too. When I lost my brother, my dearest friend, I lost memories, stories from our childhood I'll never hear again. I lost the perspective and clarity that a second witness provides in recollection. I lost life skills I'd always relied on him to demonstrate, ways of being that lay outside my nature. By all accounts I was more fun, less anxious, and more charming with him around. When he died, I didn't just lose him; I lost a part of me, a part I'd never fully get back.

When he died, I didn't just lose him; I lost a part of me, a part I'd never fully get back.

In her short story "Canary," Katherine Mansfield writes about a lonely woman grieving the sudden death of her only friend, a pet canary. She says, "When I found him, lying on his back, with his eye dim and his claw wrung, when I realized that never again should I hear my darling sing, something seemed to die in me. My breast felt hollow, as if it was his cage."[3] In a real way, one man's (even one bird's) death triggers smaller deaths in the hearts of everyone close. When a person dies we call our experience of it "loss" because in their death we are made less.

That's why I don't recognize the woman in the black-and-white photo sitting beside the fire and stockings and evergreen tree. Something about her died when that car hit the tree in the rain, and in all these fifteen years of grief, it hasn't grown back. She lives Before, and she's a different shape than I am After.

When I realized that never again should I hear my darling sing, something seemed to die in me.

When we reach for a book on grief, I think what we hope, what we desperately want to find spelled out in thick black Sharpie, is an end to the dying unfolding inside us. We want someone or something to lift the boulder off our chests, to stop the suffocating pain and enable breath. We want assurances that eventually life will be life again and not this death-ravaged husk—that one day we won't cry all the time, that we'll be capable of getting out of bed and taking showers, of going to work and cleaning the apartment and paying bills and feeding our kids meals not made in a microwave. That one day we'll pick up a new hobby or make a new friend, that eventually we'll go on vacation and actually enjoy it.

When we reach for a book on grief, I think what we hope, what we desperately want to find spelled out in thick black Sharpie, is an end to the dying unfolding inside us.

Whether or not you realize or admit it, I think that's why you put this book in your Amazon cart or picked it up off the shelf. I think you were aching for life.

If you were, *if you are*, know this: There is no returning to life before death. There is, however, life after death, life grown in the unexpectedly rich soil of grief.

There is no returning to life before death. There is, however, life after death, life grown in the unexpectedly rich soil of grief.

Endure and Embrace: A Way Through

We don't think of grief as good. It's painful. It's debilitating. It's lonely. In metaphor grief is desert, disease, or storm—destructive.

> And can it be that in a world so full and busy, the loss of one weak creature makes a void in any heart, so wide and deep that nothing but the width and depth of eternity can fill it up!
>
> —Charles Dickens, *Dombey and Son*[4]

Our inclination is to run away from it, medicate it, distract ourselves from it, or hide until it passes by.

But what if grief is good? *Or could be?*

I'm reading this book, *Grieving with Hope*, my friend Linda has recommended, when I find in it a woman whose friend has encouraged her to "lean into" grief, to "take it like waves of an ocean." Her friend advises, "Don't try to run from it. Don't try to numb it. Don't try to pretend it isn't so. It's part of your life, so feel everything. Smell everything. Be in all the moments"[5] This sounds to me like those women who say natural childbirth is a spiritual experience. I'm skeptical.

But then my wise friend Katelyn says on Facebook, "I'm not sure grief is something to rush past. It's not a sickness from which I need to recover." I wonder what she means, why anyone would want to grieve for even one minute longer than is completely necessary. She says, "Maybe grief ought to be something we learn to endure and embrace."

Endure and embrace. I hold these words in my hand, rolling them around like marbles, listening to the clink of their collision. Endurance I understand. I think of growing up in Florida on the coast, of hunkering down when the weatherman suggested evacuation. Enduring looks like staying put, braving the strong winds, mustering courage, lighting candles when the power goes out. In grief, we hardly have a choice—we can run for a while, but eventually, endure we must.

But *embrace*? What does it look like to embrace a storm? *And why would I ever want to?*

I'm staring at this question on my computer screen when I remember the late night a few years ago when, in an especially trying season and particularly dramatic mood, I stood in the middle of my street in the middle of a downpour. Tired of running from the rain, I held my arms out wide, turned my face to the sky, and cried, "God, I don't understand what's happening, but I receive it. Show me what to do with it." I said amen, and lightning like filament lit the sky.

Perhaps we embrace a storm when we realize both that we can't outrun it and that maybe there's something in it to receive.

Perhaps we embrace a storm when we realize both that we can't outrun it and that maybe there's something in it to receive.

A minister friend of mine, Tim, lost his wife to cancer a couple of years ago. My husband knew Tim to be a wise and courageous man, and so he asked Tim if he could talk on camera about the loss, about what he was doing to navigate grief. Tim agreed. In the video Tim sits at his kitchen table drinking coffee alone, telling the story of his wife's brain tumor and too-early death. He says, "I know that God does some of his best work in the desert, so I didn't want to rush through it. I didn't want to find the shortcut. I wanted to experience everything that God wanted me to experience through this."

I didn't want to find the shortcut. I wanted to experience everything that God wanted me to experience through this.

I stop here almost every time I watch the video, and I've watched it a dozen times. I wasn't wise like Tim when my brother died. I spent too many months and years pushing grief away, hiding from it, hiding it. I looked for every shortcut. I wasn't expecting God's hand in grief like Tim did, but nevertheless, despite my best efforts, I did, in my grief, find something to receive.

The idea of enduring and embracing grief assumes grief has something to offer, that in it God has plans. The person who chooses to endure and embrace grief decides that God will do with this loss what he always does with insult, injury, pain, hardship, weakness, and tragedy—he'll use it.

And we know that in all things God works for the good of those who love him, who have been called according to his purpose.

When my brother Bobby died, my mother couldn't stop quoting Romans 8:28. She said it was Bobby's favorite Scripture. I couldn't remember if it was or wasn't, and at first the words made me angry: "And we know that in all things God works for the good of those who love him, who have been called according to his purpose." All things? Really? How exactly was God going to make this death good? Good for Bobby, maybe, the hope of heaven and everything. But for me?

How could this be good for me?

Later I'd spend time reading the whole of Romans chapter 8, and I'd discover suffering like mine, worse than mine even, was the exact context of this verse. Earlier in the chapter Paul wrote, "I consider that our present sufferings are not worth comparing with the glory that will be revealed in us." His "present sufferings" included death threats and beatings, prison time, watching friends martyred for their faith. He says those sufferings are nothing compared to the transformation God is enabling in his children. Romans 8:28 says it's in the suffering that God is making things good. It's in the suffering that God is making *us* good.

I consider that our present sufferings are not worth comparing with the glory that will be revealed in us.

In the book of James, Jesus's brother opens his letter with these words: "Consider it pure joy, my brothers and sisters, whenever you face trials of many kinds, because you know that the testing of your faith produces perseverance. Let perseverance finish its work so that you may be mature and complete, not lacking anything" (1:2–4). Again, God accomplishes transformation through hard things. This time James identifies perseverance, enduring, and counting it joy, embracing, as the recommended path through pain. We could easily summarize James's message with the words "endure and embrace" in order to welcome the gift of maturity and completion.

Consider it pure joy, my brothers and sisters, whenever you face trials of many kinds, because you know that the testing of your faith produces perseverance. Let perseverance finish its work so that you may be mature and complete, not lacking anything.

This idea, that pain is the path to something better, winds its way throughout the gospels, culminating in the cross and resurrection. Jesus dies in order to live. He dies in order that we might live and be transformed into his image. Watching Jesus hang upon the cross—bloody, tired, enduring, and embracing his mission of suffering—Jesus's disciples would likely have remembered his words, "Whoever does not take up their cross and follow me is not worthy of me" (Matt 10:38). Purposeful suffering is the way to God and the way to glory. Death is a path to life.

Purposeful suffering is the way to God and the way to glory. Death is a path to life.

There's hope here if we have the stomach for it. Though we rarely return to normal after a loss and though we never completely recover, we do have the chance to let our grief achieve "for us an eternal glory" (2 Cor 4:17). In grief, we find the potential for gain, an opportunity to grow and build. While what's After will never be the same as what came Before, what's After may very well be better. That's God's promise.

Can I be frank and human for a moment? For me, that's been hard to swallow. It seems like good news—that grief could be a gift—but even if it *is* good news, you might not be ready to receive it. It might seem a little calloused to be talking about suffering this way right here in chapter 1, to so quickly label grief as a path to something better. We read passages like the ones above and wonder, "Is God saying, 'Get over it; your pain is good for you'? Or 'Drink your cup, and don't complain'?"

I don't think so, because when I see God interact with the grieving in Scripture, he's the one crying. Jesus resurrects three people in his time on earth: the son of a widow, the daughter of a Jewish leader, and one of his best friends. No one asks Jesus to resurrect the boy, but Jesus interrupts a funeral procession anyway, because he's moved by the mother's grief. Luke the evangelist describes the scene: "When the Lord saw her, his heart went out to her" (Luke 7:13). With the Jewish leader's daughter, Jesus tells the gathered crowd of mourners to stop crying because the girl isn't dead but asleep (Luke 8:52). The assumption in his words is that grieving for the dead is right and good. When Jesus raises his friend Lazarus, he famously weeps (John 11:35). He weeps not for Lazarus who he will soon bring back to life; he weeps upon encountering the grief of Lazarus's friends and family. When Jesus's own cousin dies at the hand of Herod, he withdraws to be alone and pray (Matt 14:13). Even God feels the sting and bears the sadness of loss.

Even God feels the sting and bears the sadness of loss.

God doesn't applaud when people die, already anticipating the good work of grief to come. He doesn't expect you to be happy when your loved ones die, excited about the potential of your loss. No,

God mourns with you. Death, after all, is God's enemy. Paul writes in 1 Corinthians, "The last enemy to be destroyed is death" (15:26). In the new creation described in Revelation 21, John of Patmos hears a declaration from heaven, a sort of mission statement for the New Jerusalem. Jesus, speaking from the throne, says two important things about what this new world will be like. He says (1) God's dwelling is now among the people. And (2) "There will be no more death or mourning or crying or pain."

God doesn't like loss any more than you do. Grief is the shrapnel of enemy fire, lodging itself deep in our hearts. But God, always stubborn in the face of his enemies, refuses to hand over the victory to death; so he examines the fragments of the enemy's weapon and repurposes them. He looks at grief and says, "I can do something with that."

If we'll let him, God will make something good out of our grief.

If we'll let him, God will make something good out of our grief. He won't tell us to stop crying. He'll simply ask us to let our tears water the soil of our lives, soil pregnant with potential.

In Psalm 126 I read,

> Those who go out weeping,
> carrying seed to sow,
> will return with songs of joy,
> carrying sheaves with them.

It sounds too good to be true, but I do carry sheaves and sing songs. I have gone out weeping, and I have seen a harvest of wisdom and transformation, of new life. In my grief I am less, robbed of my person. And in my grief I am made more, receiving God's gifts of grace, growth, healing, and abundant life.

I'm not glad my brother died. I'm sad—still sad fifteen years later. Just this week I was giving my husband advice on how to love his sister better and realized halfway through that I have zero experience loving an adult sibling. I burst into tears, and said, "I'm sorry. I don't know what I'm talking about." It still hurts. I still miss my brother on family vacations and on holidays. I still go to text him and remember I can't.

And yet, it's not all loss; there's gain here, too. There are gifts to be found in the valley of the shadow of death. Though loss will make you less, it can also make you more.

Here's the simple truth: You're hurting. This season of sadness is heavy and hard and you can't outrun it. So, if you're going to have to endure grief, you may as well embrace it, opening your hands to receive whatever good thing it offers. As we'll see over the course of this book, the gifts are many.

For Reflection and Discussion

1 What was your Before and After moment? Do you feel like there was a single moment of loss when you realized nothing would ever be the same? Or did loss hit you more slowly? Reflect and write about your experience.

2 Locate a picture of you before your loss. Take a moment and look closely. Who do you see when you look at that picture? How does it make you feel? Now, make two lists: one list of what things were like before your loss and one list of Afters. Be careful not to idealize the past or oversimplify the present.

3 Identify someone you know who's lost a loved one and seems to have both endured and embraced their grief. Either initiate an email correspondence or schedule a conversation over coffee. Ask questions like these: Do you feel like God is using your grief in any good ways? Has your grief led you into any new growth or wisdom?

4 Throughout this book we'll be exploring ways to endure and embrace our grief. Does the idea of embracing grief make you uncomfortable or unsettled? If so, why do you think that might be?

5 Before we move on and examine the ways God will work in our grief, do you have any questions about God's involvement in your loss? If there's anything unresolved or tense in your feelings toward God, take a few minutes to write about it. Getting your heart on paper helps you move forward with self-awareness.

6 What do you think God has for you in the desert? Have you asked yourself that question yet? Have you asked God? If not, ask it boldly: *God, what do you have for me in this desert? Empower me to receive it.*

Resources

Lewis, C. S. *A Grief Observed.*

A classic grief memoir, *A Grief Observed* is the kind of book you read with a highlighter. Lewis's observations have the ring of truth and the light of hope. As you listen to Lewis recount his experience losing his wife, you find your own struggles, pain, and questions explored with wisdom and candor.

Hodges, Samuel J., and Kathy Leonard. *Grieving with Hope.*

This simple, straightforward resource reads like a handbook for grievers. It's full of practical advice and hopeful encouragement.

2

Fighting for Life

My friend Megan and I sat on a porch in the Texas Hill Country, sun setting, friends laughing around us, sweet tea in our hands, pumpkin cake crumbs on our plates. As the crickets chirped and the kids climbed trees she told me about a loss she'd borne, about what it felt like to bear a weight so heavy. Later, she'd message me and say, "I felt like grief was crushing me, and I did not know how to have it not crush me."

Plenty of people came around Megan to support her in her pain. She never lacked for encouragement from Facebook or texts from friends. She said almost everyone validated her feelings, person after person reminding her, "There's no wrong way to grieve." But looking back she'd say, "All the validation in the world didn't help me handle it in a healthy way... I desperately wanted someone to give me a road map through grief."

"There's no wrong way to grieve." I hear that phrase a lot from friends of mourners. It's rooted in love and acceptance. It's a holy thing to say. But it's not the whole truth. And it's not wholly helpful.

SINCE MY brother died I've become something like a doula for grief, particularly for young people or people mourning tragic deaths. I'm the one friends recommend you talk to when your sister dies in a freak accident or your husband gets hit by a car. I didn't ask for this position, but I'm filling it as best I can.

Inevitably, the first question people ask me in those first few weeks and months after loss is this: "Is it always going to be this way?"

I want to say, "No." I want to grab their shoulders and lift their fallen heads and promise brighter days. I want to say, "One day you will wake up and your first thought will be about pancakes or that email or the vacation you're planning—not, as it always is now, the person you loved and lost." I want to say, "There's a whole life ahead of you, full of joy and peace and purpose."

That seems to be the answer I'm offering in this book, right? The promise of gifts in grief, the hope of something better to come? I said last chapter, "Purposeful suffering is the way to God and the way to glory. Death is a path to life."

I did say that. I believe it.

But death doesn't always lead to life. Not all suffering leads to glory. In the aftermath of death, some roads lead to more death.

Not all suffering leads to glory. In the aftermath of death, some roads lead to more death.

Consumed

When my brother died I'd never had an alcoholic drink, never smoked a cigarette or touched an illegal drug. I didn't cuss, didn't watch porn. I didn't even watch R-rated movies much. That is the context into which grief arrived. So, rifling through my files, looking for the vulnerable point of entry, grief had to grab something else. It picked food.

The problem started with a little extra grazing at the funeral meal, popping chicken nuggets like Xanax, a second helping of the cake someone dropped off, ordering pizza because I didn't feel like cooking, then ordering a bigger pizza and cinnamon sticks. Eventually I'd eat an entire basket of chips at the Mexican restaurant waiting for a friend or a whole bag of snack-sized Reese's cups. Together my husband and I would plow through a pan of lasagna meant to feed eight.

> The concept that time heals is probably responsible for more heartache than any other single wrong idea in our society.
>
> —John W. James and Russell Friedman, *The Grief Recovery Handbook*[1]

Overeating is not an unnatural response to sadness. Some people stop eating while grieving. Others never stop eating while grieving. So it was "natural" and "understandable" to be eating all the food.

But natural and understandable don't equal healthy, and natural and understandable don't equal productive. Gluttony doesn't stop being gluttony because you're grieving. In fact, when you're grieving all the consequences of gluttony are enhanced, because you're vulnerable.

If food had been drugs or alcohol or sex, surely someone would have stepped in to stop me. But eating was my booze, and thirty pounds later (on a twenty-one-year-old's metabolism) I'd be forced to come to terms with the effects, not just weight gain, not just fatigue and low self-worth, but also an inability to embrace my feelings without reaching for an edible distraction. Food gave me something to hold in my shaking hands, a hit of delight to dull the despair, and a way to pass the time. Eventually overeating would teach me to listen to my flesh and open the door to chronic failings in self-control. All that fat and sugar would also partner up with my sadness and bully me into a depression that would never fully go away.

> I do not believe that sheer suffering teaches. If suffering alone taught, all the world would be wise, since everyone suffers.
>
> —Anne Morrow Lindbergh, *Return to the Sea*[2]

What started out as sadness at the loss of my brother spiraled into an addiction, and my choices after my brother died would shape the next ten years of my life. Those choices would also have a direct impact on my ability (inability, really) to receive what grief had to offer.

Tipping Point

Every loss is an inciting incident, the point in the story when the action starts. Grief forces us out of habits and routines, upturns our normal, and demands new choices. When I was a little girl and my grandmother died I felt like I'd been blindfolded and spun, unable to put a tail on a donkey, let alone adapt to my new school, new room in my grandfather's house, and newly grieving, largely distracted parents—all consequences of her early death. One day I was eight and in second grade making a Christmas list and baking cookies, the next I was wearing pantyhose and sitting quietly in the corner at a funeral home on Christmas Eve.

Grief forces us out of habits and routines, upturns our normal, and demands new choices.

Newton proved that an object in motion stays in motion with the same speed and in the same direction unless acted upon by an unbalanced force. Death is an unbalanced force.

Newton proved that an object in motion stays in motion with the same speed and in the same direction unless acted upon by an unbalanced force. Death is an unbalanced force.

When her mom died, Wren didn't know who to tell. Years before, she'd been adopted by her aunt and uncle. Her college friends didn't know she had a mother other than her aunt. She tried not to bring up her past too often, complicated and checkered as it was. Her mom was an addict who couldn't raise her. What was there to tell? But now, sitting beside her mother's still-warm body in the ICU, she felt alone. She'd try to share the news on Facebook, but people would get confused, think her aunt had died. She took the post down and went back to school like nothing happened. And everyone else acted like nothing happened, too.

Wren was new to Christian faith when her mom died. Before the loss she didn't feel close to God, not exactly (though she suspected she should). After, she felt even more removed. Feeling unseen, she started lashing out at the people closest to her. She took to drinking too much, started a sexual relationship with a guy who already had a girlfriend, cut ties with friends. All of it was so much easier to fall into within the fog of grief.

The same thing happened to Grace. Grace had dutifully cared for her grandfather throughout his Alzheimer's journey, and when he died she felt spiritually adrift in her grief. A couple of years later when her grandmother died, she'd fall off the edge of a cliff. She'd let her anger go unchecked, push people away, and slip into a sexual addiction that led to sexual abuse. She said even now, years after that dark season, years into a healthier life and anchored faith, "I still have this exact same reaction with a major loss. I first think Oh, alcohol can take this away. . . . Then I start thinking I should just find a random man."

After Nick's dad died, his mom became an alcoholic. Nick, feeling unattended and unmoored, said he felt "led by fear." He told me, "The fear ranged from little things, like being unusually and irrationally afraid of the dark on camping trips with my friends, to big things, like having sex with my girlfriend . . . because I wanted to experience all of her before she could die unexpectedly. That carried into our marriage, and we were unhealthily codependent for years because I was so afraid she would die suddenly when we were not together." Every car ride, every work trip, wrought nightmares as fear suffocated.

Chad's grief over the loss of his sister (and the court's decision not to give him custody of his sister's children) triggered a latent mental illness. Early on, Chad convinced himself that his sister hadn't actually died. He said it was the only way he could cope. In the first six weeks after his sister's death, he told me, "I drank, smoked weed, got a tattoo, and had an ongoing affair."

Chad said grief turned him into a completely different person. He wrote to me, "Death changes us."

It does. Or more precisely, death requires change. After loss, we cannot remain on the same road.

> But grief makes a monster out of us sometimes . . . and sometimes you say and do things to the people you love that you can't forgive yourself for.
>
> —Melina Marchetta, *On the Jellicoe Road*[3]

Two Roads

Before Jesus died on the cross, Judas was already dead. He'd hung himself on a tree, such was his guilt. Guilt, grief—they're intertwined here. Judas lost a friend and a teacher when Jesus died. He lost a man he'd lived with for three years, a man who held Judas to standards no one had before, a man who opened Judas's eyes to things, things he saw clearly too late. In the end, Judas's reaction to his betrayal of Christ reveals his confidence in Christ's identity and his devastation at his inability to stop the crucifixion. Judas's suicide is the kind of choice humans make in the aftermath of death. Judas got too close to death, and it ate him. That happens. You've seen it.

Peter, though, responds to death differently. While Peter's betrayal of Jesus is perhaps less consequential, Peter's love for Jesus is undeniably greater. His disappointment in himself must have been crushing. When Peter denies his Lord and dear friend, he weeps, and then, tears still wet on his face, he repents. A few hours later, Jesus lying in a tomb, Peter (like Judas) will face the debilitating cocktail of guilt and grief. When Jesus dies, Peter will weep again, surely, but Peter (unlike Judas) won't try to escape. He'll stick around to endure and embrace the pain.

Judas breaks under his grief. Peter bears up under it.

Eventually Jesus will return. Peter will be forgiven. And Peter will serve a primary role in the institution of the church and the growth of God's kingdom of earth.

For Judas, death led to death. For Peter, death led to personal resurrection.

Death undeniably propelled both Peter and Judas into change. The loss of Christ made them different men. For Judas, death led to death. For Peter, death led to personal resurrection.

Why the difference? What did Peter have that Judas didn't?

Do I want to live? Or do I want to die?

There's no easy answer, but part of the answer has to be the will to live. After watching their friend die, they each had a choice, two paths: Do I want to live? Or do I want to die?

See, here's what the force of death, enemy of God, tells you in your grief—death tells you to despair, to believe in the perpetuity of darkness and the persistence of pain. Death tells you to be afraid, to live a little life, dangers and risk backing you into cramped corners, blocking you from the life just beyond your tentative reach. Death tells you you're alone. It cuts you off from the love, support, and strength of your community. It isolates you from wise voices bringing life. Death makes you doubt your faith, doubt God's

> You could grieve endlessly for the loss of time and the damage done therein. For the dead, and for your own lost self. But what the wisdom of the ages says is that we do well not to grieve on and on. And those old ones knew a thing or two and had some truth to tell, . . . for you can grieve your heart out and in the end you are still where you are. All your grief hasn't changed a thing. What you have lost will not be returned to you. It will always be lost. You're left with only your scars to mark the void. All you can choose to do is go on or not.
>
> —Charles Frazier, *Cold Mountain*[4]

goodness, doubt God's presence, eventually even doubt his very existence. Death makes you selfish, convincing you to indulge your every urge no matter how it affects the people around you. Death says stay on the couch, ignore your kids, quit your job, turn on the TV, say whatever you want, take what's yours. Death hooks you on a drug or drink, porn or food or Facebook. Death distracts you in any way possible from the one thing it least wants you to do: live.

Death distracts you in any way possible from the one thing it least wants you to do: live.

After executing your loved one, death, sensing your vulnerability, will come for you next. Will you let him have you?

Will you surrender to death or will you fight death and be changed by God?

Will you do whatever feels good and become someone you don't recognize and don't respect? Or will you lean on the power of Christ to enable new life in you?

Will you quit or will you weather this grief and welcome God's work of transformation?

Will you endure this storm? Or will you let it destroy you?

Will you endure this storm? Or will you let it destroy you?

For so many of us, drowning in grief, this is the most important question we'll answer. Our decision will affect everything.

We say there's no wrong way to grieve, and if we mean everyone grieves differently, cry as much as you need to; don't try to be someone else, sure. That's wise. But if we mean all roads lead to healing, we're wrong. My friend Megan sensed this when she asked for a roadmap. She realized grief had brought her to a crossroads and here she would need to make a choice. Which way should she go?

Grief had brought her to a crossroads and here she would need to make a choice. Which way should she go?

A few years ago, my friend Joy and her husband Stephen lost a baby girl. Born with brain damage, never able to breathe outside of life support, their baby lived inside a hospital for twenty-six days. They named her Maggie. If she hadn't died, Maggie would have turned seven this year. My friend Joy took birthday cake to the grave. And cried.

> Deep grief sometimes is almost like a specific location, a coordinate on a map of time. When you are standing in that forest of sorrow, you cannot imagine that you could ever find your way to a better place. But if someone can assure you that they themselves have stood in that same place, and now have moved on, sometimes this will bring hope.
>
> —Elizabeth Gilbert, *Eat, Pray, Love*[5]

Joy told me recently about how hard it was at first to hold back the tide of grief, to stop the raging, destructive flood. She said, "I had to ask myself, 'Am I going to let this consume me?'" She decided she wouldn't.

Joy and Stephen shared their story of grief with our church, and as she told us about the moment when doctors first saw signs of trouble on a blurry ultrasound image, she said, "That's what started this horrific journey that somehow led us closer to God." A big part of that "somehow" was Joy's decision not to be consumed. Once she planted that flag, the way forward became clearer.

> At times the fact of her absence will hit you like a blow to the chest, and you will weep. But this will happen less and less as time goes on. She is dead. You are alive. So live.
>
> —Neil Gaiman, *Sandman: Fables and Reflections*[6]

We are not powerless in grief, slaves to death and our basest desires. No, we can find power in grief to deny those desires, power located in Christ's presence and movement and the hope it provides. If enduring and embracing grief means we're buoys in a stirred-up sea, receiving the waves, it also means we're anchored to something, something flexible but stable and fixed.

What comes after a loved one's death, how our lives shake and shift post quake, won't depend as much on the force exerted as it will upon the object of that force. What happens depends on you, your posture of defiant endurance, and how tightly you're tied to your anchor.

We are not powerless in grief.

For Reflection and Discussion

1 Are you being consumed by grief? Do you feel like there's anything you could do to loosen grief's stranglehold on your life? If you're up for it, write the following sentence in your book or

> Offer yourselves to God as those who have been brought from death to life.
>
> —Romans 6:13

on an index card or with Sharpie on your hand: I choose not to be consumed.

2 What have been the negative ways you've seen grief affecting you? First, remember to give yourself grace in this season; making decisions of any kind is hard in grief. Willpower is remarkably hard. Second, ask yourself, "Why am I turning to this destructive thing or behavior?" Are you trying to run away from grief? Are you dulling it?

3 Do you want to build a new, joyful life? Or are you feeling like giving up? Make a list of "reasons to live" and a list of "reasons to give up." To be clear, we're not talking about suicide here (though that may be something you're thinking about—if so, I hope you'll reach out to a friend, counselor, or loved one). Rather, we're talking about closing down your life like you might a store at 9:00 p.m., refusing to keep going or trying. What reasons do you have to do that? Reflect on both lists. You might even share them with God in prayer.

Resources

Jose, Stephanie. *Progressing through Grief.*

The main reason I recommend this workbook (essentially a grief journal) is the list titled "Your Rights in Grieving." It's excellent, good to copy onto an index card and tape to the bathroom mirror.

James, John W., and Russell Friedman. *The Grief Recovery Handbook.*

The intensity of this book is a little much for me, but I do appreciate James and Friedman's desire to lead people out of grief by confronting grief. If you're a person who responds to systems and plans, this may be just what you need to find healing.

3

Practicing Hope

Dina's brother died on her last day of intensive therapy. She'd been admitted for emergency mental health intervention on the day her friend Debbie died, and now, just a few weeks later, here she was receiving more unbearable news. A tractor had rolled over on her brother at work. Her parents picked her up, and the three of them drove ten hours to see his body and plan a funeral.

When the call came about Dina's brother I didn't believe it. I'd walked with Dina through her recent struggles and therapy, met up with her at the facility where she'd been admitted, prayed over her, tried to provide loving accountability in her relationships and vices. In the last few weeks, since she'd started seeking help, I'd seen so much progress in her. And now, one more terrible, heavy thing hefted onto her already-sagging shoulders—it was too much.

But a month later, with Dina sitting on the couch next to me at our church small-group gathering, I realized I'd been wrong. This last death hadn't been too much. It had been just the thing Dina needed to bring her all the way home.

Dina's brother dying served as a sort of flare, alerting the people around her, many of whom had no idea about Dina's suicide attempts or addiction, that she needed help. Help rushed in from every direction. Soon she was surrounded, held, and empowered by family, friends, and her church, these people like lanterns lighting the way.

Grief woke Dina up. She said, "I remembered I'm still alive, and I shouldn't be, and it made me realize things needed to change."

In a very real way, Dina's brother dying saved her life.

I OFTEN hear this story, variations of it anyway. A person is flailing, a loved one dies, and suddenly they find perspective. Or a person is living a safe, predictable life and a loved one dies and now they realize life is short and they need to get out and really live. We said last chapter, loss demands change. Sometimes that change looks like destruction, devastation, or despair, but often grief inspires powerful positive change, change that begins with a decision to live and blooms in endurance.

What good has grief borne in your life?

Recently I asked friends a question: What good has grief borne in your life? One friend who lost two babies to miscarriage said grief taught her to be less selfish, to stop thinking only of herself and her personal pain. Another, whose best friend died of colon cancer at thirty-four, said grief taught him, finally and fully, that he wasn't in control. He wrote,

> No matter how much I loved and tried to hold onto my friend, he still died. No matter what I say or do, I will lose things. I will grieve those things. Because I am not in control. It's one thing to say you're not in control as a child of God. It's a whole 'nother ballgame to experience it.

I had another grieving friend tell me, "God is teaching me that I'm stronger and braver than I ever knew, and with that strength and courage, little by little I'm pushing myself to do the things I always wanted to do and to answer hard questions that I would never even entertain in the past."

On Tuesday nights I lead a group of people who're new to faith in conversations about God. Last night I asked, "What circumstances or

As an exercise in hope, post the question 'What good has grief borne in your life?' to your Facebook page or Twitter feed. While other people's gifts in grief don't fix your pain, they do provide hope that perhaps one day there will be some good in your grief, too.

people or experiences contributed to your growing belief?" I heard stories about altar calls, answered prayers, Scripture, and provision.

When Carmen's turn came around, she talked about her grandmother. She said, "When she was dying, I'd say 'See you tomorrow,' and she'd say, 'Si Dios quiere.' *If God wants*." Carmen laughed, "Everything was 'Si Dios quiere.'" After her grandmother's death Carmen remembered that inspiring faith and began to build a faith of her own.

As I rifled through my own experiences that night, looking for reasons to believe in God, looking for the pillars of my own faith, I noticed how many of those pillars were erected during the years directly after my brother died. What circumstances contributed to my growing belief? Grief did. For me, grief was the wrecking ball that both tested the strength and merit of my most fiercely held beliefs and forced me into new construction—not just of beliefs but also of practices and character. Persevering through grief grew me.

We boast in the hope of the glory of God. Not only so, but we also glory in our sufferings, because we know that suffering produces perseverance; perseverance, character; and character, hope.

That is, after all, what Paul the apostle promised, that suffering has merit and usefulness. He wrote, "We boast in the hope of the glory of God. Not only so, but we also glory in our sufferings, because we know that suffering produces perseverance; perseverance, character; and character, hope" (Rom 5:2–4).

I don't often hear people say of Christians (or *to* Christians either) that we "glory in our suffering." But here it is in Scripture, an invitation to let suffering be an opportunity, a gift. Paul says suffering grows things inside us. Good things. Things we want. And so, why wouldn't we stand with open hands, ready to receive whatever grief has to offer?

To endure and embrace grief isn't a passive task.

Possibly because it's not as easy as it sounds. To endure and embrace grief isn't a passive task. We don't wait around and let it happen, standing slack-jawed like a surprised Cinderella at her magical, fairy-godmother transformation. Consider the metaphors we've used so far:

- Riding waves like a buoy in the ocean
- Standing in a storm
- Journeying through a desert

Each one requires active participation in order to ensure survival. The buoy fights to stay in place though battered, tossed, and beaten by the waves. The news anchor reports by the shore in a hurricane, fighting the wind and hail to simply stand. Tired and thirsty, the desert traveler takes one step after another, pushing through the heat and pain, hunting an oasis.

I won't sugarcoat the truth; in order to receive gifts in our grief, we're going to endure quite a lot of pain, more than we're able to withstand on our own. Like the buoy in the ocean, to survive we'll need an anchor.

In order to receive gifts in our grief, we're going to endure quite a lot of pain.

How to Keep Going

In the last chapter we looked at Peter and Judas, two men responding to grief and regret in two different ways. We saw that, when confronted with a crossroads, Judas gave up, and Peter kept going. Judas chose death, and Peter chose life. Choosing death makes a lot of sense in the throes of grief; it represents an end to the pain, a way out. Choosing life takes wisdom, courage, and the nerve to persevere, knowing the circumstances won't be easy. How do you muster that kind of nerve? Looking at Peter, I think the answer must be hope.

After Jesus died, Peter didn't run away. He didn't go home to his wife, to his comfortable bed. Instead, despite the possibility of arrest, he stayed in Jerusalem (see Acts 1 and 2). Maybe he stayed close

> Imagine you're Peter. What would you have done after your friend and teacher died? What seems strange to you about Peter's behavior? What makes sense?

because he didn't know what else to do. Likely he stayed close because he wasn't ready to give up.

When Jesus rose from the grave and the women came to tell the news, Peter ran to the tomb. He jumped up from his seat and sprinted. When he arrived, his friend John hesitated outside the tomb, but not Peter. He walked right in. And when he saw the linen that once wrapped his friend, his friend now unwrapped and unshackled, hope stirred to life.

The first time we see a detailed account of Peter encountering the risen Christ, Peter's in a boat (John 21:3). He's been fishing all night with no catch. A man yells from the shore, "Throw your nets on the other side." Peter and his friends do what the man says and the nets fill to teeming.

This advice to tired fishermen and these empty-turned-full nets—it's all a sort of inside joke, a reminder of a previous moment, a time Jesus had done the very same thing, a time he'd made a promise about who his apostles would become. John sees the hint and says, "It's the Lord." Peter hears John, throws on his clothes, and jumps in the water (v. 7).

This makes perfect sense. The one who jumped out of a boat to walk on water, the one who refused foot-washing from his savior, the one who first confessed the messiahship of Jesus, Peter is impetuous and passionate. This is his nature. Also, Peter's friend is on the beach. Peter's friend who died. Wouldn't you jump out of the boat to swim to your dead friend?

But in another way, this doesn't make much sense. Doesn't Peter know Jesus died on a cross? Doesn't he know death is permanent? Would you jump out of a boat just because someone said your dead friend was on the beach? Or would you be angry and sad at the cruelty of the joke?

And suppose Jesus has been raised; isn't Peter ashamed to meet him? Doesn't he remember the last time he and Jesus locked eyes, betrayal still wet on his lips?

Why does Peter jump out of the boat?

Hope.

Why does Peter jump out of the boat? Hope.

Years after Peter swims to shore and eats breakfast with Jesus, after he's preached the first post-resurrection sermon, baptized the first gentile, and helped build the church in Jerusalem, Peter will sit down at a table, pull out the first-century equivalent of a pen, and remembering the taste of fish and the smell of fire and the sound of waves lapping up on the shore, he'll write about a gift he received from his friend: "Praise be to the God and Father of our Lord Jesus Christ! In his great mercy he has given us new birth into a living hope through the resurrection of Jesus Christ from the dead, and into an inheritance that can never perish, spoil or fade" (1 Pet 1:3–4).

Peter had a living hope, unfailing confidence that what's to come is better than what is. Peter believed there was more life ahead of him. He believed this hard thing could lead to some new good thing. Peter believed in the possibility of resurrection—Jesus's and his own, here and to come.

The writer of Hebrews said, "We have this hope as an anchor for the soul, firm and secure" (6:19). When the waves crash and the wind whips, when everything conspires to undo you, it's hope that holds you steady. In the desert, when you can't imagine one more step, when you're tired and hungry, hope is the bread of endurance.

We have this hope as an anchor for the soul, firm and secure.

In your grief, if you believe, truly believe, that what's ahead is good, you can find the strength to keep going.

In your grief, if you believe, truly believe, that what's ahead is good, you can find the strength to keep going.

What Hope Is Not

Before we go any further with hope, before you discount my assurance that hope is the only way to endure and embrace grief,

> We remember before our God and Father your work produced by faith, your labor prompted by love, and your endurance inspired by hope in our Lord Jesus Christ.
>
> —1 Thessalonians 1:3

the enabler of perseverance and the anchor in transformation, perhaps we need a list of things hope is not.

Hope is not optimism.

Hope is not optimism. An optimistic person believes good things will happen because he wants good thing to happen. Hope isn't based on what we want. It's based on what we've been promised.

Hope is not fragile.

Hope is not fragile. Emily Dickinson says "'Hope' is the thing with feathers," because it lifts and soars. Hope, though, is not like a sparrow or cardinal or canary, hollow-boned and flighty. Hope is hardy. If it's a bird, it's a working bird. Hope is like those eagles that snatch goats off mountainsides. It's sturdy, capable of great acts of strength, the kind of thing you take into battle.

Hope is not a luxury.

Hope is not a luxury. Hope isn't just for those who can afford it. Hope is for the desperate, dissatisfied, broken, and aching. Hope is for people who need rescue, a way out, a cure, an escape plan. Hope is an all-in bet.

Hope is not a placebo.

Hope is not a placebo. Hope isn't a Jedi mind trick, fooling yourself into happiness, putting off your sadness for some other day you never let come. Hope effects. Hope rewires, reroots, reshapes. Hope catalyzes chemical change. Hope empowers feats of extraordinary endurance.

In grief, hope is your daily bread.

In grief, hope is your daily bread.

Proof

I have a friend who's having trouble carrying a baby to term. Every failed pregnancy, every lost child, leaves her more convinced she'll never hold a baby in her arms. Hope is hard to muster in light of the evidence. While hope is the help we most need in grief, the sustaining force in our efforts to receive whatever grief might offer, it's in grief that hope can be hardest to trust.

> "You can't eat hope," the woman said.
>
> "You can't eat it, but it sustains you," the colonel replied.
>
> —Gabriel García Márquez, *No One Writes to the Colonel*[1]

Hope says what's to come is better than what is. *Or what was.* Loss says the exact opposite thing. After a loved one's death, we can't help but think,

- I'll never be as happy as I was.
- I'll never have another child.
- I'll always be lonely.
- I'll never find as good a friend.
- I'll always be angry.
- I'll never be able to support myself like she supported me.

It's in grief that hope can be hardest to trust.

When it's your child in the coffin or your wife or best friend, it's hard to argue with the voices, hard to believe something better might be coming. Grief seems to say, "Your best life is in the past." And that feels true.

Grief seems to say, "Your best life is in the past."

Hope says, "Your best life is in the future." I wonder, "How can you be so sure?"

Hope, as we mean it in this book, is certainty in the promises of God, primarily the promises of future glory, both on earth and in the life to come. As I see it, two promises emerge in Scripture as the ideal fuel for enduring grief. First, we find hope in the promise of an end to our suffering and a forever life with God.

Paul writes in 1 Corinthians 15:19, "If only for this life we have hope in Christ, we are of all people most to be pitied." He's arguing for the resurrection, confident that a future rebirth into an eternal kingdom is the destiny of God's people. He writes later, excitement dripping from his words, "For the trumpet will sound, the dead will be raised imperishable, and we will be changed. . . . When the perishable has been clothed with the imperishable, and the mortal with immortality, then the saying that is written will come true: 'Death has been swallowed up in victory'" (15:52–54).

Death has been swallowed up in victory.

This isn't a dream. It's a promise. This is our future.

Be strong and take heart, all you who hope in the Lord.

—Psalm 31:24

Though I suffer every day before that day, I will still have hope, because that day is coming and that day will be better, immeasurably and infinitely better, than today.

This isn't a dream. It's a promise. This is our future.

To the grieving, the idea of a coming victory over death lifts and inspires. For years I've read Paul's words as a sort of William Wallace or Henry V front-line battle cry. I imagine the mortal clothed with immortality, my enemy death overthrown, and I'm recharged, encouraged, sent forth, inspired to keep on living. I remember my suffering isn't permanent, that one day it will end, and the hope of that end makes the suffering preceding it a noble burden.

There's of course a double gift in God's resurrection promise—a finish line for suffering and a new beginning for my dead. Hope says one day my brother will be pulled from his coffin and wrapped in new flesh. Hope says one day my grandmother's lungs will fill with new breath. Hope says one day my miscarried children, rejected in pieces of muscle and tissue, will be welcomed and made whole. Hope says one day my grandfather, teller of stories, will have new stories to tell. Though I suffer every day before that day, I will still have hope, because that day is coming and that day will be better, immeasurably and infinitely better, than today.

The second great hope we find empowering us in grief is our hope in God's ability and commitment to strengthen and shape us in his image here and now. In other words, we have hope God will make us better.

Paul writes in Colossians 1:27–29, "To them God has chosen to make known among the Gentiles the glorious riches of this mystery, which is Christ in you, the hope of glory. He is the one we

Imagine Resurrection Day. Try to put yourself in the moment. Who do you want to see raised to new life? How do you think you'll feel? Write yourself a note as a reminder when you're feeling overwhelmed by grief.

"When you come out of the storm, you won't be the same person who walked in. That's what this storm's all about."

—Haruki Murakami, trans. Philip Gabriel, *Kafka on the Shore*[2]

proclaim, admonishing and teaching everyone with all wisdom, so that we may present everyone fully mature in Christ. To this end I strenuously contend with all the energy Christ so powerfully works in me." God at work in me, a burgeoning glory expanding within me, a full maturity in Christ—these are promises for the child of God, promises provoking me to open my hands in seasons of grief, even when it's hard, even when I'd rather run and hide. I can receive grief because I know God will be faithful to use it to achieve my transformation.

God at work in me, a burgeoning glory expanding within me, a full maturity in Christ—these are promises for the child of God.

Philip Yancey writes in his book *Where Is God When It Hurts?*, "As we rely on God, and trust his Spirit to mold us in his image, true hope takes shape within us, 'a hope that does not disappoint.' We can literally become better persons because of suffering. Pain, however meaningless it may seem at the time, can be transformed."[3]

As we rely on God, and trust his Spirit to mold us in his image, true hope takes shape within us, "a hope that does not disappoint."

Grief hurts. You wake up in the morning and find it piled on your chest. You go to work and find it caught in your throat. You sit beside a friend and find it leaking from your eyes. You push aside your dinner plate, having found it in your gut. For a while, grief is everywhere and in everything.

Hope helps. Hope helps you lift the pile. It helps you find your voice. Hope helps you dam the tears (a bit). Hope helps you take a bite. Everywhere and in everything, hope shows up, lifting our eyes, lifting our hearts, lifting our very selves in character and kind.

Everywhere and in everything, hope shows up, lifting our eyes, lifting our hearts, lifting our very selves in character and kind.

Living Hope

This book is about how to receive what grief has to offer. Hope is the how—practical hope, living hope, hope with dirt under its

> The very least you can do in your life is to figure out what you hope for. And the most you can do is live inside that hope. Not admire it from a distance but live right in it, under its roof.
>
> —Barbara Kingsolver, *Animal Dreams*[4]

fingernails. Grief bears gifts, though often they come in unlikely forms. Hope, like a pair of glasses, helps us see what we couldn't see without it. Hope empowers us to consider our circumstances and in them find a way to grow and be blessed. Hope sees anger and suggests lament. Hope sees loneliness and advises connection. Hope sees longing and gives thanks for what is.

Hope, like a pair of glasses, helps us see what we couldn't see without it.

In the following chapters we'll consider ten behaviors prompted by grief and enabled by hope. We'll explore what it looks like to learn from our grief, to listen to it, to see what it stirs up and what it helps us remember. We'll stand in the storm, welcome the rain on our cheeks, and say, "I receive this grief. Show me what to do with it."

> Grief does not change you. . . . It reveals you.
>
> —John Green, *The Fault in Our Stars*[5]

For Reflection and Discussion

1 What does it mean to "glory" in your suffering? On a scale of one to ten (ten being insane), how crazy does that seem to you right now? Why did you pick the number you did?

2 How have you defined hope in the past? How would you define it after reading this chapter?

3 Which of the two kinds of hope are you most convinced of—the hope of resurrection one day or the hope of transformation now? Which one do you find most inspiring in your efforts to endure grief? How certain are you of these two promises? Practically speaking, what could you do to grow your hope?

4 What does hope demand of us in grief? What does it provide for us in grief?

5 At this point in the book, what are your expectations? What are you hoping to learn? What are you hesitant to embrace?

Resources

Yancey, Philip. *Where Is God When It Hurts?*

When, in the aftermath of grief, I first began struggling with God's goodness, Yancey was the author I turned to. In his books I found wise, honest, thoughtful counsel that led me into deeper, more grounded faith.

Wright, N. T. *Surprised by Hope.*

Though the title reads like a grief resource, this book is actually an argument for active engagement in God's efforts to expand the reign of his kingdom on earth. I include it here, because sometimes in focusing on the hope of heaven we can miss the hope of transformation on earth.

4

Exploding Safely: The Gift of Lament

At my brother's funeral I stood at the front of the church in a black dress with a starched white collar and made jokes. My brother had been a humor writer for our college paper; I edited his work (and got him the job). In his memory, in front of so many of his faithful readers, I'd decided to write one last column, from him to us. It was sentimental and silly and just what a twenty-one-year-old might write on an occasion like this. I told his friends to "borrow" silverware from the school cafeteria for bracelet-making (something he'd done on multiple occasions) and pretend to fall down crowded stairs once a day (another of his habits, usually holding an ice cream cone). I said these things would help us remember him, and in our laughter, we did. I made it through three minutes without crying and sat down quickly, joy still dancing in the air. I realize now that my words were just the kind of words Bobby would have shared had the roles been flipped—reaching for humor like body armor, hoping the crowds didn't notice the tears for the laughter.

No one told me I shouldn't cry at the funeral. Family and friends expected little from me and provided much for me. My parents cried freely and courageously in my presence. I had every reason to feel safe expressing my hurt in the context of all this love. But I realize, looking back, it wasn't about them. It wasn't rejection or embarrassment I feared. It was the feelings that made me afraid. Anger, abandonment, guilt, and despair churned in the deepest parts of me, whispering plans for my destruction. I wanted so much to keep them there, down deep, contained. What would happen if they surged up and over my carefully constructed walls? What might this pain, acknowledged, do to me? Was there a safe way to explode?

In the coming days I would, in fact, explode, feelings flung against the walls, anger like bullets shot, pain wrecking, despair in the wreckage. And in that explosion I would discover that while the feelings are dangerous and not at all safe, they're less dangerous on the walls than they are in the deep. I'd also learn that the best place for exploding is in the presence of God.

Was there a safe way to explode?

Cooped Up

Recently I spent some time with a teenager mourning his sister's death in a tragic accident. He took a bite of blueberry scone, and crumbs fell into his lap as he recounted the 911 call and the bystander's disinterested description of the flames. Not a single emotion crossed his face. It wasn't that he didn't have any. Or that he'd healed from the pain. I knew enough to know the pain was hiding, hidden.

He told me he was struggling to connect with his mom. His girlfriend wanted to break up with him but felt bad for him and wouldn't. He never talked to his old friends. He hadn't been to church since the funeral. Every relationship became defined by distance. Grief, this grief he didn't want to talk about, this grief he thought he'd stuffed away, had become a thick wall, standing between him and everyone, including and especially God.

Grief, this grief he didn't want to talk about, this grief he thought he'd stuffed away, had become a thick wall, standing between him and everyone, including and especially God.

He'd decided to join me for breakfast, because he was finally ready to talk about it, and he preferred to start with a stranger, a stranger who might understand how he felt.

After Bobby died I didn't want to talk about it. What was there to say? I didn't know how to answer a question like "How are you?" in the foyer after church or at the fridge on my lunch break. *How am I?* Every day bore a different answer, but never was the answer polite, measured, or appropriate for general audiences. I kept the real answers to myself. "Fine," I said. "Surviving," I quipped. "Thanks for asking," I said through forced smiles. I didn't want to burden people with my pain and anger. I didn't want to depress my friends. I didn't want to mess up a perfectly good day. I didn't want sympathy or pity. I didn't want whatever awkward response they'd give to my too-thorough or too-personal or too-sad answer. Whatever came out of my mouth would be wrong. And whatever came out of their mouth would be wrong, too. That's what I thought. And that's why I held it all in.

With no password to set the feelings loose, I kept them cooped up inside, scratching at the door, gnawing at me.

David Biro says in his book *The Language of Pain*, "Language and pain seem as far apart as the opposite poles of an electric current. While language can capture much of the diverse range of human experience, it fails us in the case of pain."[1] That's how it was. Even for me, a professional communicator with a degree in language, there were no right words to describe the pain. With no password to set the feelings loose, I kept them cooped up inside, scratching at the door, gnawing at me.

> To weep is to make less the depth of grief.
>
> —William Shakespeare, *King Henry VI*, Part 3

I wish someone had told me what I learned later on, the thing I told this boy across the table at breakfast. I told him, "You can talk to me. I want you to. But you really need to talk to God. He's much better at this than I am."

Out Loud

The oldest book in the Bible and perhaps the oldest book in the world is the book of Job, the story of a man who loved God and lost everything. It's a chronicle of his grief and the way grief upended all he thought he knew about life and God. In it, Job wrestles with God's identity, sovereignty, and goodness. It's a hard book to read—hard because it's emotional and hard because it's, frankly, all over the place. Job sounds like a man who's grieving. He doesn't always make perfect sense. He whines, dragging his sadness behind him like a millstone. He's confused, wrecked, angry, and disconsolate. He says, "Why did I not perish at birth, / and die as I came from the womb?" (3:11). He cries, "Sighing has become my daily food; / my groans pour out like water."

Sighing has become my daily food; / my groans pour out like water.

What I find most interesting about all of this is the fact that Job was God's first story, likely the first holy Scripture to be written down. What does it mean that Scripture begins with a grieving man pouring out his broken heart to his Creator? It must mean something. In my grief it means something to me.

A lament is "a weeping." And the Bible is full of laments.

Later in the history of God's people, songs like Job's were grouped into a collection called the Psalms. While the Psalms include all kinds of prayers, songs, and sentiments, close to half of them (sixty-five to sixty-seven, depending on how you count) are labeled "laments." Lament, as it's used in Scripture and as it's used to categorize Scripture, means "grief or sorrow expressed in complaints or cries." A lament is "a weeping." And the Bible is full of laments.

Consider lines from this one (Psalm 42) penned by King David, a man well acquainted with grief and hardship:

> My tears have been my food
> day and night.
> Why, my soul, are you downcast?
> Why so disturbed within me?
> I say to God my Rock,
> "Why have you forgotten me?
> Why must I go about mourning,
> oppressed by the enemy?"
> My bones suffer mortal agony
> as my foes taunt me,
> saying to me all day long,
> "Where is your God?"

Why have you forgotten me?

David's lament psalm (this is only one of many) is marked by pain, raw emotion, confusion, vulnerability, and honesty. We feel David's pain here. Maybe we've felt this way ourselves standing beside a casket or walking through the automatic doors of the hospital, breathing fresh air for the first time in days, wishing we had someone to go back in and see.

Why must I go about mourning?

Lament says, I'm not going to ignore or numb myself to the fact that things aren't right.

We've felt this way, but many of us have never said words like this aloud. Afraid to look them in the eye, we've held back. In a sermon on the power of lament, my husband Justin said, "Lament says, I'm not going to ignore or numb myself to the fact that things aren't right." Lament is an exercise in receiving grief, embracing it by expressing it.

The lament Psalms, along with the book of Job, the book of Lamentations, parts of Revelation, sections of the histories, and other huge swaths of the Bible, show us that pain is best experienced out loud. Held in, grief rots the bones. Anger and despair grow like mold in the dark, taking root in our hearts, holding us captive. Our brooding silence pushes us away from every person who might love us. But spoken, those feelings lose much of their power. In the light they can be clearly seen, considered, and weighed. They become points of connection instead of walls of separation.

Job's lament (and David's) free me to speak. Even though I might speak wrong, even though I might speak words wet with despair, even though I might sound like a complainer or a doubter or a weakling—still, I should speak. I read these words in this holy book, and I find comfort and an example.

The Right Audience

I haven't always had great luck telling people about my pain. Maybe you haven't either. The few times I've mustered the courage to share something raw and unmeasured in grief, I've found people either startled by my candor or quick to reproach my lack of faith or

> Maybe if you're angry with God now and then you're normal. Maybe that's part of being the people of God.
>
> —Peter Enns, "When God Is Unfaithful: Reclaiming a Theology of Lament"[2]

understanding. It's particularly a problem with those inexperienced with loss. So often I feel like a person in a pit yelling up to people looking down, my words and theirs garbled by the distance.

What I realize as I read lament is that David's words, Job's words, Jeremiah's in Lamentations, they aren't addressed to people, people who might not understand, people who might not care. Lament has one primary audience, and that audience is God. When we hurt, God is the one best equipped to receive our complaint.

In a sermon on Psalm 42, David's psalm of lament that we looked at earlier, Katherine C. Kerr reflects on the famously mysterious line: "Deep calls to deep / in the roar of your waterfalls." She says this idea of deep calling to deep, essentially David in his pain calling to God in his gravity, is rooted in the human desire to be understood in our pain. She says,

> We find ourselves in the depths. Down there, in the depths of pain and loss and abandonment, we can't help but look back up through the murkiness to the surface, remembering what it felt like up there in the sun. But the view is obscured and the friends who wave at us from those heights look almost like ghosts, so distorted and hazy are their well-wishes by the distance we feel from them and the reality of our circumstance.

She says, "From the deep, it is hard to connect to the surface. But in the deep, we are never alone."

David knows, even when no one understands his grief, God does. Even when no one is left to hear his complaints, God will.

In Romans chapter 8, the apostle Paul writes about Christians waiting for the resurrection, about the difficulty of it, the way our souls yearn for something better and beyond. He says while we're here waiting, "the Spirit helps us in our weakness." How does it help? "We do not know what we ought to pray for, but the Spirit himself intercedes for us through wordless groans. And he who searches our hearts knows the mind of the Spirit, because the Spirit

So often I feel like a person in a pit yelling up to people looking down, my words and theirs garbled by the distance.

Lament has one primary audience, and that audience is God. When we hurt, God is the one best equipped to receive our complaint.

From the deep, it is hard to connect to the surface. But in the deep, we are never alone.

intercedes for God's people." When we're weak, when we can't find the words, when we find plenty of words but they don't all make sense, when our words are coated in vitriol and vinegar, the Spirit intercedes. He takes our accusations and questions and demands, all ill-translated by us from feelings into words, and translates them back into the language of the heart, the language we all speak (us and the Spirit and the Father), the language of wordless groans.

Is there a safe place to explode? Yes. With God.

Lament brings the mess to the person best able to deal with it. God welcomes our pain. He listens to it. He honors it. He understands it. And he'll lead us to make some sense of it when there's sense to be made. Is there a safe place to explode? Yes. With God.

A Plan for Yelling

> Our pain can serve a higher purpose if our pain leads us back to God.
>
> —Esther Fleece, "5 Things You Need to Know about Lament"[3]

When I pray lament prayers, and I pray them rather often, I follow the pattern I find in the Psalms:

First, I complain.

I say, "God, things are bad." In my grief I tell God how much I miss the person I loved. I tell him I feel robbed. I tell him I feel abandoned. I say, "This isn't how it should be." I ask him why he didn't let my person live. I ask him why no one seems to care about my pain. I complain until all the complaints are scattered across the ground, like leaves fallen from shook trees.

Second, I ask God for help.

"Save me," I say. Lift me up. Light this darkness. Heave the burdens from my shoulders if only for a moment; help me catch my breath. I ask God to give me hope, to help me persevere. Some days I ask him to come back soon. Some days I ask him to let me die. Some days I ask him to let me live. Always I ask him to leverage his unlimited power on my behalf.

Laments often end there, at least ours do. But David's laments don't. Neither do Job's. Theirs push beyond desperation and into the realm of trust and hope. The third movement of a lament is affirmation of faith and confession of hope. It's when we say, "God, things are bad. Save us." *And*, "We know you can. We know you will." Here, recognizing the audience of our rant, we lift our eyes and remember who God is and what he's promised. Job will say, "I know that my Redeemer lives, and at the end he will stand on the dust." David says in Psalm 43 (part b of Psalm 42 in the Hebrew collections of the Psalms), "You are God my stronghold." He ends both 42 and 43 with the words, "Put your hope in God, / for I will yet praise him, / my Savior and my God." Even in the middle of their darkest pain, even as they accuse God of playing a part in their anguish, Job and David rely on him expectantly.

We know you can.
We know you will.

When I pray a lament prayer, these last two parts don't always come easily. Sometimes I want to sneak out at intermission before trust and hope come traipsing onto the stage, expecting something of me. But when I stick around, I find trust and hope providing much more than asking. Like dropping an anchor, speaking words of true trust and hope steadies the boat in the turbulent sea.

Like dropping an anchor, speaking words of true trust and hope steadies the boat in the turbulent sea.

Sometimes I have to catch a glimpse of God before I can jump into faith. Sometimes glimpses are hard to grab, and so I hunt him down and stare. Maybe I'll read Scripture and watch God be God on the behalf of his people. Maybe I'll parrot a Psalm, "The Lord listens to the needy and does not despise his own." Maybe I'll seek and count the promises. Maybe I'll ask a friend to tell me about a time when God showed up with light in the middle of their darkness. Maybe I'll pull out a journal or a photo book and look for his movement. Once I've seen him clearly, I'll be enabled to trust and hope.

So, third, I praise my able God.

I say, *God, I see all you've done. You're powerful. I look at my life and see your hand. You're faithful. God, I trust that you have what it takes to save me. And I have hope that, just as you've saved others and just as you've saved me before, you will save me again.*

It's here in this last part of the lament where I'm realigned. This is the place where I stand back and look at the two piles I've made, one a heap of all that's wrong and broken, one a mountain of God's proven power. Both are bigger than I am. One is bigger than the other.

Take about twenty minutes to write a lament psalm. It doesn't have to be pretty, but do try to follow the form: (1) God, things are bad. (2) Save me. (3) I know you can. I know you will.

Out here in the light, our feelings of anger, guilt, despair, and loneliness aren't small or benign. But they are known, measured, and shared by a God who can (and will eventually) lift them.

Lover's Quarrel

There are plenty of reasons to avoid God in grief, the most obvious being that we blame him for what happened. And even if we don't blame him, we still wonder why he didn't show up the way we wanted him to. How do you talk to God about your disappointment with God? What if the thing you're lamenting is God's failure to be who you needed him to be?

How do you talk to God about your disappointment with God?

As we've noticed already, David and Job both go to God even as they identify him as the source of their pain. David and Job both accuse God of absence, unfairness, and delaying in keeping his promises, and David and Job both still seek him out as comforter and savior. Why? I think because they loved him.

Recently, after listening to a grieving friend talk about her blooming doubts and questions, I asked what she was doing to find answers. She shrunk in her chair, a little embarrassed that she wasn't doing much other than skipping church. I said, in the kindest way I knew how, "If you're mad at God, tell God. People in a committed relationship don't run away when things get hard. They stay and argue." Silence will push you away from God, but striving connects you to him.

People in a committed relationship don't run away when things get hard.

Lament is a lover's quarrel. And while it can be contentious, the very act of turning to God instead of away from God brings you closer to him, even if you're yelling accusations. My husband says to concerned mourners, "Lament is more an act of intimacy than it is an act of distance." You don't question someone you don't believe exists. You don't passionately accuse a stranger. Lament is proof of relationship.

As I look back on the past fifteen years of grieving my brother, I can't help but point to lament as one of the great gifts of grief. It was grief that brought me to God in anguish, unable to contain my hurt anymore. I dragged myself into his presence and detonated the bomb tucked into my deepest parts. What I discovered was a safe place to explode, and in exploding, I found understanding and love.

Lament is a lover's quarrel.

For Reflection and Discussion

1 Are you trying to bury, hide, or contain your grief? If so, why do you think that is? How is it making you feel? What concerns do you have about the possibility of giving voice to your feelings? If not, what are you doing to express your grief? How's it going? What hurdles are you facing?

2 Would you prefer to talk about how you're feeling to a friend, to a counselor, in prayer or in a journal? Why do you think that is? What makes you feel safe with that person or in that space?

3 Do you have any reservations about turning to God in lament? If you don't feel close to God right now, try one of the following prompts to begin a conversation (write in response to the prompt for as long as you can):

> God, I blame you for . . .
>
> God, I'm not sure you're real anymore, because . . .
>
> God, I don't want to talk to you, because . . .

4 Do you struggle with the third movement of lament? What would it look like for you to stare at God? Where could you go for reasons to trust him?

Resources

Billings, J. Todd. *Rejoicing in Lament: Wrestling with Incurable Cancer and Life in Christ.*

In this autobiographical book, Billings explains how the lament Psalms enabled him to understand and process his grief. Billings's faith is remarkable (sometimes in a way that made me feel inadequate but never in a way that made me feel judged). The gift of this book is in Billings's ambition to grieve well and in his offer of the lament Psalms as a vocabulary for the grieving.

Gerhardt, Justin. "Lament." Sermon, http://www.rrcoc.org/lament.

If you're new to lament, this sermon is a moving, aching argument for the power and beauty of the practice. Gerhardt says we've neglected lament and models how we might integrate it into our worship of God. This sermon will give you the permission you need to approach God in pain. Grab tissues.

5

Welcoming Help: The Gift of Belonging

Within an hour of the first phone call to the first friend on the morning my brother died, a tsunami of help descended on my family, soaking us in love, surrounding us in care. People did the normal things like bring food, plan a funeral meal, and write kind notes in sincere cards. They did other things too, things I wouldn't have expected people to do. My uncles drove with my dad to claim Bobby's car and clean up his stuff from the side of the road. Someone put up a cross at the crash site. People asked where they could donate money, and my parents created a scholarship fund; tens of thousands of dollars poured in. Some people still give every year. One of the things I remember thinking seemed strange was a delivery of paper plates, trash bags, paper towels, toilet paper, and plastic forks. It must have felt weird to walk into a grieving person's house with a twenty-four pack of Angel Soft toilet tissue on your arm, but it turned out to be the most practical gift. To this day, I always bring toilet paper to the house where the mourners gather. They'll need extra.

BOBBY DIED in December, less than six months into my husband's first job as the preaching minister at a tiny congregation of God's people in the middle of nowhere, Alabama.

They hardly knew us. We hardly knew them. As the months unfolded, this grief of ours would prove to be both a hurdle and a bridge to relationship.

The morning Bobby died, before we drove to the airport and got on a plane and spent weeks in Florida with our family (paid time off well beyond the contractual allowance), I remember Ron Little, an elder, standing in my living room while I cried, still dressed in my pajamas, no makeup on my face. He didn't know me well enough for this; he didn't know what to do or say, what would give this twenty-one-year-old girl peace. I remember he was kind, and I remember he was there. But I also remember wishing he would leave. The vulnerability of this brokenness was too much.

Before he left that morning, Ron asked what we planned to do with our Christmas presents. I looked toward the tree, packages spilling from under the lowest branches, and froze. I had no idea what to do with those presents. Presents were item 562 on my list of concerns. Ron said, "Let me take care of it." So we did. And on Christmas Eve, when my family gathered to celebrate and exchange gifts, I had gifts, because Ron had mailed them to my parents' house. It wasn't a great Christmas. We all cried more than we laughed. But the gifts were a grace—small joys, pricks of starlight in a pitch-stained sky.

The vulnerability of this brokenness was too much.

When we returned to Alabama after the long trip and the first, most tragic waves of grief, our church tried to help us, but I noticed quickly that I wasn't good at receiving help. Blame it on my Enneagram number (1) or my Myers-Briggs type (INFJ) or my sometimes-crippling introversion, but I think probably I was proud and I didn't want people to think I was weak. On Sundays I pretended to be strong. I taught Bible class and sat on the second pew. I did my hair and makeup and always wore dresses or slacks. On Sundays I seemed fine. On all the other days I hid in my house crying, eating gas station pizza, and watching bad TV. They didn't

They didn't know how much I was hurting, because I didn't want them to know. I wanted them to think I was strong.

> The root of all virtue and grace, of all faith and acceptable worship, is that we know that we have nothing but what we receive, and bow in deepest humility to wait upon God for it.
>
> —Andrew Murray, *Humility*[1]

know how much I was hurting, because I didn't want them to know. I wanted them to think I was strong.

I hear this kind of self-reliance in grief is normal. We want to carry our own load, fix our own problems, heal alone in a cave, thank you very much. The early help isn't bad. We'll let the ladies fill our fridge with casseroles if it makes them feel good. But it's that meddling, later help that makes our stomachs turn. It's the people who stick around and keep giving, the people who want to give more than we're comfortable receiving, the people who've seen more of our weakness than we're comfortable with them seeing. We push those people away. We do it by rejecting their help, and we do it by pretending we don't need their help.

We want to carry our own load, fix our own problems

Turns out, even one day a week of pretending is too hard. Eventually my grief started to show, and people noticed and started trying to help. I kindly said, "Thanks anyway." I rejected dinner invitations, offers for conversation over coffee. I said no to every kind of help. Fortunately, they wouldn't be stopped by my pride. One day after a storm had blown some shingles off our roof, my husband and I came home from work to find the roof repaired, no explanation. Another day we found new flowers planted in our beds. Someone mowed our lawn. Kind old ladies brought us tomatoes and squash. Someone gave us an old car to drive, so we'd have two. Friends invited us to play cards once a week (and chased us down to be sure we didn't flake out). Later they'd take us out on their boat where water, sunshine, and silence would work wonders in healing our souls. We'd stay at that church in Alabama for three years, and for three years they would patiently and persistently force themselves into our lives, breaking down my pride with one intrusive gift after another.

They would patiently and persistently force themselves into our lives, breaking down my pride with one intrusive gift after another.

Grief isn't something we want to endure alone. And at the same time, grief *is* something we try to endure alone. We know we shouldn't stay home on the couch. We know we can't hold all of our feelings in. We know our lives will fall apart if we don't accept the meals or the help getting the kids to school or the check to pay for the coffin. But still, for many of us, the idea of welcoming help seems weak, awkward, attention-seeking, uncomfortable, or needy. We don't want charity or pity.

Charity, though, just means love. And not wanting love is probably a problem.

It's possible grief will lead you into public vulnerability for the first time in your life. If so, the help that almost inevitably comes will teach you something. Needing another person's help (despite our desire to go it alone) may be initially unpleasant, but as we'll see, it's one of the great gifts of grief.

Belonging

In Romans chapter 12, the apostle Paul gives a short summary of what it means to belong to the body of Christ. He says, "For just as each of us has one body with many members, and these members do not all have the same function, so in Christ we, though many, form one body, and each member belongs to all the others" (v. 4).

Paul tells the church in Rome, *You're not on your own. You need others, and others need you.* Paul's words remind us that no one is strong or whole alone. It's in connection that we find life, purpose, identity, even capability.

Skip ahead a few verses and you'll find him speaking directly to mourners, or more precisely *about* mourners. He tells the church, "Rejoice with those who rejoice; mourn with those who mourn."

For many of us, the idea of welcoming help seems weak, awkward, attention-seeking, uncomfortable, or needy. We don't want charity or pity.

Charity, though, just means love. And not wanting love is probably a problem.

You're not on your own. You need others, and others need you.

> It's strange how much emphasis we place on the art of giving, with none at all on the more intricate grace of receiving. Of course, grace of any sort is as difficult to come by these days and as impossible to hoard as untrodden snow, but it may be that this particular grace is the least accessible of all. It requires us to abandon, at least for a few minutes, our sense of ourselves as strong, self-sufficient, generous, supportive—and unworthy—human beings.
>
> —Joan Gould, "On the Graceful Art of Receiving Gifts"[2]

When loss knocks and grief sneaks in the open door, it's God's people who come alongside us (or at least ought to come alongside us) to share in our pain. They come because they belong to us. They come because we belong to them.

When loss knocks and grief sneaks in the open door, it's God's people who come alongside us (or at least ought to come alongside us) to share in our pain.

Grief, too heavy for individual lifting, helps us see what should have been obvious before, but perhaps wasn't. We weren't made to live life alone.

Grief, too heavy for individual lifting, helps us see what should have been obvious before, but perhaps wasn't. We weren't made to live life alone.

Recently a friend of mine lost his father. When out-of-town family wanted to come and stay in his father's home for the funeral, he didn't know what to do; his father had been a hoarder, and the house was crammed with trash. In hours, a crew of friends from his church had gathered to clean out the house, clearing out rooms stacked with knickknacks and empty plastic food containers, washing sheets and dumping clothes into bags to take to Goodwill. I was there that day, and I watched my friend's face, a strange mix of love and shame coloring his cheeks. It was hard to welcome fourteen people into his dad's room, embarrassing to watch them pull dirty food plates from under the bed and ball up soiled sheets. At the same time, I saw gratitude in the tears in his eyes—how beautiful it must have been to be loved and served like that. Soon the house was clean. And my friend didn't have to be embarrassed anymore. His out-of-town aunts and cousins never saw the mess. Love covered it up.

Grief is an introduction to the skill of accepting love and belonging. Grief opens us to the kind of dependence God intends for us both in our weakness and in strength. When we're grieving we *must* accept help. So often there's no other way forward. Later, because of the grieving and because of the help, we'll find ourselves more willing to belong.

Grief is an introduction to the skill of accepting love and belonging.

Paul writes again in 1 Corinthians 12 about the body: "Just as a body, though one, has many parts, but all its many parts form one body, so it is with Christ . . . there are many parts, but one body." Next, Paul writes,

> The eye cannot say to the hand, "I don't need you!" And the head cannot say to the feet, "I don't need you!" On the contrary, those parts of the body that seem to be weaker are indispensable. . . . God has put the body together, giving greater honor to the parts that lacked it, so that there should be no division in the body, but that its parts should have equal concern for each other. If one part suffers, every part suffers with it; if one part is honored, every part rejoices with it. (vv. 21–26)

It's true; we can't say we don't need each other. Trying to go it alone won't work. Eyes need hands and hands need feet and feet need veins and veins need lungs and lungs need tongues. We belong to each other. When I'm weak and you're strong, I'm made strong by your strength.

If one part suffers, every part suffers with it.

We belong to each other. When I'm weak and you're strong, I'm made strong by your strength.

I write this chapter as a minister, the wife of a minister, the granddaughter of a minister. I find myself entangled in body life. I know everyone; everyone knows me. And though sometimes that entanglement brings trouble, most often it bears delicious fruit. I speak about community and belonging from a place of privilege. You may not be so lucky. You may be feeling removed from the body, perhaps especially in your grief. Maybe your person died with no tsunami of help knocking down the door. Maybe you've borne this pain alone, without a second pair of strong shoulders to bear up under the load and lighten your share of the burden. Maybe this second grief, the realization of your solitude, is as heavy as the first.

For some, this coming to terms with the consequences of your independence is not a surprise. You've never intentionally pursued connection with a spiritual community and now, finding yourself entirely disconnected and alone, you realize why so many people around you suggested you should. You need help, but you don't have a network to help you. To you, I'd say, It's never too late. Now is as good a time as any to find your people. Find a group and bind yourself to them. Lash yourself to the mast, come what may. If that's the only good thing to come from this grief of yours, you'll have found a most precious gift.

Now is as good a time as any to find your people. Find a group and bind yourself to them. Lash yourself to the mast, come what may. If that's the only good thing to come from this grief of yours, you'll have found a most precious gift.

What do you do if you thought you belonged to a community and find out you don't?

For others of you, this solitude is surprising, because you thought you were connected to a body, but lately you're not so sure. You keep waiting for someone to notice you, waiting for someone to reach out, but no one does. What do you do if you thought you belonged to a community and find out you don't? When perceived life and real life don't match up, how do we mind the gap? Here are a few suggestions:

- Believe the best. Sometimes the people around us simply don't know how to help. Sometimes they don't realize we need help. Sometimes they're neck deep in pain of their own.
- Reach out first. Sometimes we need to depend upon others before they explicitly offer. That's okay in the body of Christ. Legs don't wait for permission from the brain to depend upon the brain.
- Lament disappointment. Sometimes people will legitimately let you down. It's not okay when the church on earth doesn't live into its heavenly image, so pray like David did, bemoaning what is, asking for what's been promised.
- Repent. Sometimes the reason you feel alone is that though you've been going to church, you haven't been belonging. You haven't depended on anyone, and you haven't been someone upon whom other people depended. Let this be the moment you decide to change that.
- Seek help outside an unhelpful community. If your church isn't going to be the body you need, seek help outside it. You'll find God's people in a counselor's office, at work, on Facebook, and in your family.

Full Circle

A few years ago, I went back to that church in Alabama for Ron Little's wife's funeral. Donna died rather suddenly—a brain tumor, cancerous. She and her husband had served that church for decades, devoted their lives to the body. She fed people, held them in their pain, taught their children in Bible class. She sang alongside them in worship, her faltering soprano an octave above her husband's baritone, leading him as he led the church in song. I stood in the back at first, in the foyer, watching Ron by the casket. I picked up a handwritten card from a stack on the table and examined the words, obviously Donna's loopy script. She'd made these for years, cards printed on white computer paper, cards for members to use and share. How many of these cards of encouragement had I received in the season of my most intense grief? So many. And though the cards had been from a dozen different people, every one bore Donna's hand. I suspect each of us in the building on the morning of Donna Little's funeral had either sent or received one of those notes.

Ron and Donna Little had been strong when we were weak. And now, with Ron mourning Donna, we gathered around to be his strength. We knew just how to help, because we'd watched him (and her) help us.

In grief, we learn how to belong in the body. We learn how to be weak from firsthand experience, being thrown in the deep end of the pool, and we learn how to be strong from watching those who lift us up. Among the many ways grief shapes a person, perhaps the most beautiful is the way it fuels empathy and compassion, the way it opens our eyes to another's pain, the way it compels us to go to Costco and buy too much toilet paper and too many trays of deli sandwiches. Grief is a permanent-marker reminder inside us that people need help. Later, when we need help less, we'll see that reminder scrawled on the walls of our memories, and if we'll walk fully in our identity as people of hope, we'll find the people around us who need help and we'll help.

We learn how to be weak from firsthand experience, being thrown in the deep end of the pool, and we learn how to be strong from watching those who lift us up.

Grief is a permanent-marker reminder inside us that people need help.

For Reflection and Discussion

1 Do you struggle to accept help? If so, why do you think that is?

2 Is there anyone trying to help you who you've rejected? Consider reaching out and confessing your reluctance to accept.

3 Are you a part of a church community? Have you been playing an active role in that community? Is it a good place to find help? Is there something you need to do to better plug in and belong?

4 When have you been weak and been blessed by someone else's strength? When have you been strong and blessed someone who was weak?

5 What have you learned in your grief that could be helpful to others?

6 Have you noticed any growth in empathy or compassion in yourself? If so, share an example. If not, pray asking for God to lead you into greater empathy and compassion.

Resources

Sittser, Jerry. *A Grief Disguised*.

Perhaps the best book I've read on grief, Sittser's story of wading through the loss of his wife, mother, and daughter in one tragic accident is wise, compassionate, and thoughtful. Sittser's example of welcoming help from friends and family moved me and reminded me of the power of helplessness to create connection and belonging.

Simon-Thomas, Emiliana R. "How to Open Yourself Up to Receiving Help." https://tinyurl.com/y79nzqwx.

Part psychological explanation for our hesitancy to accept compassion from others and part argument for the practice of self-compassion, this article reoriented me and gave me one good step toward growth.

Amodeo, John. "5 Reasons Why Receiving Is Harder Than Giving." https://tinyurl.com/yb3zklkq.

This quick, simple read works as a kind of diagnostic tool for identifying what it is that's keeping you from receiving the help you need. Read it and see if any of the five reasons Amodeo offers hit home.

6

Living in the Present: The Gift of Daily Bread

It happened in a yellow cab in Manhattan at Christmastime, white lights dancing on the hoods of passing cars, honks in the streets, "All I Want for Christmas" on the radio. I sat in the backseat with two out-of-town friends; my husband sat up front. We'd been to dinner at our favorite place, and now we were headed to the Rockefeller tree. Friends, good food, and fifty thousand colored lights—a perfect night.

But something was wrong. All night I'd felt off—tired and moody. Now, I found myself bent over with stabbing pains in my abdomen. I apologetically bowed out of the rest of the evening, told my husband I was fine, and exited the cab on an empty corner a borough away from my apartment. Standing in the snow, waiting to cross the street and grab the R train home, I felt the blood run down my leg.

We told our parents about the baby over Thanksgiving, a week before this moment in the snow on the corner. We'd waited for seven long years to have kids. Our moms and dads cried, called every relative, overloaded my dinner plate, and told me a hundred times to sit down and relax. Telling our parents made the pregnancy real. When we arrived back in Brooklyn, we spent our evenings shopping in cute boutiques for organic baby blankets and hipster onesies.

The night I miscarried in the cab—that's what it was, a miscarriage—I took a local train, climbed four flights of stairs, unlocked two deadbolts, and brushed past our tiny, plastic Christmas tree on my way to the bathroom and then the bed. Under the tree, the only present already purchased was a small, star-covered cotton sleeper.

MISCARRIAGE GRIEF is a strange kind of grief, because in it you mourn the death of a future, an anticipation never realized. Mourning this baby whom I'd never held, with a gender I didn't yet know, and no name to speak aloud in lament confounded me. *How could it hurt so much to lose someone you've never met?*

I'd only known about the baby for three weeks, but already I'd imagined his blond hair and blue eyes and chubby baby cheeks. Already I'd taken him to Coney Island to play in the surf. Already he'd won speech contests like I did. Already he played guitar like his dad. Already he'd played safety on the high school football team. Already I had grandchildren clamoring for space on my lap.

When I lost the baby I lost more than just the baby. I lost the life I'd imagined with that baby turned boy turned man. The grief was harder, heavier, because I'd been living in the future.

I say miscarriage is a strange grief, because miscarriage doesn't look back so much as it looks ahead. But maybe all grief finds its most painful expression in looking ahead. Maybe the most difficult loss to bear is the loss of memories imagined but not yet made.

Maybe all grief finds its most painful expression in looking ahead. Maybe the most difficult loss to bear is the loss of memories imagined but not yet made.

That's how it's been, grieving my brother. For me, the hardest moments are the times when my mind hits fast forward, and I realize he's nowhere to be found . . .

> *When I imagine my children being born and their uncle not being there in the hospital room with bubblegum cigars*
>
> *When I realize I'll never take another family vacation with Bobby, that my kids won't learn to swim with his kids, that we'll never again shop for road-trip candy or sing along to the radio*
>
> *When I consider taking care of my parents as they age, when I watch my mother care for her dying father alongside her three brothers, and I imagine doing that same thing on my own*

What imagined memories are you grieving? Make a list of three or four future dreams you lost when you lost your person.

It's too much, this future empty of him. I don't have the strength to carry it—this pile of Bobby-less tomorrows. It's too heavy. But that hasn't stopped me from trying, breaking my back under the weight of disappointment.

Loss reminds us that we do not have the final word.

—Jerry Sittser[1]

Robbed

Most people who grieve experience some measure of anger. Sometimes our anger is rooted in an unresolved past. Often it's rooted in what we perceive to be a "stolen" future. Pastor Andy Stanley says, "The root of anger is the perception that something has been taken. Something is owed you."[2] For mourners, what's been taken is both our loved one and the future we expected with that loved one.

The root of anger is the perception that something has been taken. Something is owed you.

My friend Kelly was furious when her sister died unexpectedly. Just thirty years old, she died too soon. For Kelly, her death represented more than the loss of a sister; her sister's death represented the loss of *her* future. Kelly and her sister were best friends. They texted every day. They took vacations together. They made plans. Every time Kelly imagined tomorrow, her sister was there. When Kelly's sister died, it was like death reached down and snatched up her whole life. Looking ahead to days, weeks, months, and years without the sister she loved, Kelly felt robbed.

Looking ahead to days, weeks, months, and years without the sister she loved, Kelly felt robbed.

No one would argue with Kelly; she *was* robbed. Death stole her sister. And for that, death deserved her holy rage. But while she *was* robbed of her sister, she *wasn't* robbed of her future. That's because the future was never hers to begin with. All those plans she made, all those expectations she had, she never had a right to them in the first place.

That sounds harsh. It sounds harsh when James, the brother of Jesus, says it, too:

> Now listen, you who say, "Today or tomorrow we will go to this or that city, spend a year there, carry on business and make money." Why, you do not even know what will happen tomorrow. What is your life? You are a mist that appears for a little while and then vanishes. Instead, you ought to say, "If it is the Lord's will, we will live and do this or that." As it is, you boast in your arrogant schemes. All such boasting is evil. (4:13–16)

According to James, we are temporary people given to vanishing. Assuming we'll live and breathe, even assuming our friends and family will—that's a boast. An arrogant, evil one.

Why, you do not even know what will happen tomorrow. What is your life? You are a mist that appears for a little while and then vanishes.

I don't think Kelly thought of it that way. I'm sure she didn't. I don't think that in imagining a future with her sister she was consciously putting herself in the position of God, believing arrogantly in her own ability to control what comes. I think she just forgot we're mist. I think she forgot today isn't a certain indicator of what tomorrow will bring. I think she forgot that anything might happen, that the future is unpredictable and untamable. I think she forgot, because I did. I forgot that death hides behind corners, and I assumed I'd live. I assumed my brother would live. I assumed my baby would, too. I lived a life built on assumptions, and when those assumptions proved a foundation of sand, much of my life washed away.

We are temporary people given to vanishing.

These days, thanks to my experience with grief, I assume much less. Seeing a twenty-year-old boy die, miscarrying and then miscarrying again, it'll convince you that you don't know what's coming. And while it's a scary realization at first, it's one of the most helpful gifts of grief. The hard-won perspective of grief endured is this: we don't know what all the future holds, and so we hold the future lightly. There's freedom in a loose grip.

The hard-won perspective of grief endured is this: we don't know what all the future holds, and so we hold the future lightly. There's freedom in a loose grip.

A few years ago, my husband Justin and I traveled across the country for a bucket list hike. It's one of those hikes you read about in magazines, the kind you train for. On this particular trail, you'll find signs with the number of people who've died on it. It's dangerous and exhilarating and worth every uphill step.

> And what does your anxiety do? It does not empty to-morrow, brother, of its sorrows; but, ah! it empties to-day of its strength.
>
> —Alexander Maclaren[3]

Before we went, Justin and I updated our will. We made sure the kids had a place to go, made sure the insurance money went to the right people. We called a friend to tell him where the documents were on our way to the airport. On the plane, sitting beside two friends who'd come along, both new to hiking, we mentioned something about the will and the hassle of getting a notary. Our friends' eyes widened, and one of them asked, "How dangerous is this hike?"

I don't remember how we responded, but maybe we said something about being mist. Maybe we said, "If the Lord wills, we'll survive." We make people uncomfortable with the things we say these days.

At lunch with my parents a few weeks ago, sitting on a patio eating French fries, I said offhand, "When I die, I want to be buried in one of those hippie cemeteries that don't allow coffins. Just wrap me in a blanket and put me in the ground. I'd like it if you'd plant a tree on top of me."

My mom nodded while she finished her bite. She took the opportunity to chime in and remind my dad and me of her plan to be cremated and scattered in Central Park. She said, "I know it's illegal, but figure it out." My dad asked for burial at sea.

Grief reminds you life is short. Grief removes all illusions of safety and assurance. Grief says, "You can't count on tomorrow," and grief helps you remember you're not in control.

We said these things sober over lunch. Pass the ketchup.

Grief reminds you life is short. Grief removes all illusions of safety and assurance. Grief says, "You can't count on tomorrow," and grief helps you remember you're not in control. All of these truths sound terrifying. But somehow, they're not. They're gifts.

The "somehow" comes when you see through the lens of hope, confident in the promises of God. There's plenty you're not promised, but there's also plenty you are. No, you're not in control. But God is. No, you may not live to see tomorrow. But you'll live forever with God. Yes, death may steal your loved one. But God will walk beside you in your grief and God will enable a future reunion. What's been stolen will be returned. What's been planted in the cold ground will bloom into new, glorious life.

The future isn't all unknown. It's not all uncertain. There are some things we can anticipate with absolute assurance, and they're the best things, the things that bring life and freedom. As the Proverbs writer said, "There is surely a future hope for you, and your hope will not be cut off" (23:18).

No, you're not in control. But God is. No, you may not live to see tomorrow. But you'll live forever with God. Yes, death may steal your loved one. But God will walk beside you in your grief and God will enable a future reunion.

Too Heavy

When grief opened my eyes to the possibility of loss and pain, a possibility I hadn't yet understood or entertained, I first responded with overcorrection. I went from never expecting it to always expecting it. I did what I'd done before and projected my present experience onto my future. However I felt today, that's how I'd certainly feel tomorrow. If I woke up in the morning feeling sad and tired, aching and lonely, I figured I'd always wake up sad, tired, aching, and lonely. The thought of a lifetime of sad and lonely mornings was just too much to handle. So I'd climb back in bed, the weight of fifty years' future grief tucked like a lead blanket around my buckling shoulders.

The thought of a lifetime of sad and lonely mornings was just too much to handle.

Yet again, my pain originated in eyes that wouldn't stop looking ahead, eyes trained on the farthest speck of future I could see. It's this future orientation that crushes us in grief. The future, particularly a future we cram with pain and sadness, is too much to carry.

> Never, in peace or war, commit your virtue or your happiness to the future. Happy work is best done by the man who takes his long-term plans somewhat lightly and works from moment to moment 'as to the Lord.' It is only our *daily* bread that we are encouraged to ask for. The present is the only time in which any duty can be done or any grace received.
>
> —C. S. Lewis, *The Weight of Glory*[4]

It's this future orientation that crushes us in grief. The future, particularly a future we cram with pain and sadness, is too much to carry.

Give us this day our daily bread.

This prayer reminds us, we depend on God and God provides enough. But only enough for now.

There's this principle God begins to teach the Israelites after they've escaped from slavery in Egypt and before they enter the promised land of Canaan. It's a principle wrapped in a practice, the practice of receiving daily bread.

The Israelites need food, and food in this wilderness is hard to find, especially for so many mouths. God, as he has done already and will continue to do, provides what they need. But the way he provides it is most unusual.

"Then the Lord said to Moses, 'I will rain down bread from heaven for you'" (Exod 16:4). He means this literally. Every day, bread will fall from the sky and rest on the grass like dew. God says, "The people are to go out each day and gather enough for that day." He specifies that they collect enough for *only* that day and not an ounce more. Some people will try to gather too much, but God will make it spoil.

The Israelites depend on God for bread like this, daily bread, for forty years. Every morning Israelite men and women will wake to an empty pantry. And every day, they'll eat.

A few hundred years later Jesus will teach his apostles to pray and he will say, "Pray like this," providing a prayer of example, a cheat sheet of sorts for struggling pray-ers. Sandwiched in that prayer for the coming kingdom, forgiveness, and deliverance we find the line, "Give us this day our daily bread" (Luke 11:3). Surely he means literal bread. He means for us to have what we need and to be content with it. But also I suspect Jesus is getting at something like what God was getting at with the bread from heaven. This prayer reminds us, we depend on God and God provides enough. But only enough for now.

I was at Chick-fil-A with my friend Janine, both of us tired young moms, overextended, buried in the requirements of adulthood, when Janine, who was also enduring a painful season of grief, said, "It's too much to carry." We talked about how hard it is to look ahead and know things will never be the way we expected them to be. How difficult it is for her, for instance, to wake up in the morning alone knowing she'll likely wake up hundreds more times with no one in the bed beside her.

But then it was like a light shone down on our booth, illuminating our chicken nuggets and the pile of pain we'd heaped on the table. And we started talking about daily bread and the Israelites and the Lord's Prayer.

As we looked back on the long seasons of loss we'd each experienced, we realized God had gotten us through everything in our path. He hadn't lifted the load entirely, but he had made each day's load bearable.

What we wanted was for God to carry tomorrow's sadness today. We wanted him to give us enough strength for all the days ahead right now, so we might carry the whole future in one go, like my husband bringing groceries in from the car. We wanted a pantry full of manna. But what we needed was exactly what Jesus had told us to pray for, enough for today. Just today.

What we wanted was for God to carry tomorrow's sadness today.

Janine only needed the strength to wake up alone today. Tomorrow, if she woke up alone, she'd pray again.

Each day has enough trouble of its own.

In the Sermon on the Mount, Jesus told the poor, struggling, anxious people spilling across the grass at his feet, listening to his every word, "Do not worry about tomorrow, for tomorrow will worry about itself. Each day has enough trouble of its own" (Matt 6:34).

This is the key to enduring grief we so frequently miss: Each day will have trouble. Live one trouble at a time. In other words, bear today's grief today. And leave tomorrow's grief for tomorrow.

This is the key to enduring grief we so frequently miss: Each day will have trouble. Live one trouble at a time. In other words, bear today's grief today. And leave tomorrow's grief for tomorrow.

Will the next ten years of grief be hard? Maybe. Maybe not as hard as I think. Maybe I'll experience some unexpected joy that lifts my grief. Maybe I'll die and that will be the end of that. Maybe I'll make a friend who becomes a brother of sorts. Maybe he'll throw my kids in the air and tell them stories about Jesus. Maybe

I'll be in an accident that wrecks my memory and I won't even remember my brother. Maybe Jesus will come back. Wouldn't that be wonderful?

I don't know what tomorrow will be like. It might be full of trouble like today. But it's trouble I can deal with when I get there. Today has trouble of its own, trouble I'll tackle with Jesus.

What does it look like to practice the principle of daily bread in our everyday grief? It looks like refusing to chase rabbits, refusing to let your thoughts wander into the coming years, weighing down the days with grief. It looks like being intentionally present. Taking one step at a time, celebrating today's victories without worrying you'll undo them tomorrow. It looks like choosing sobriety today. Choosing joy today. Choosing to wake up today. Choosing to get dressed today. Knowing that you only have to make decisions for today.

God promises daily bread, daily filling, daily sustaining, daily life.

There's power in that.

You can make the next right choice. You can do the next hard thing. God promises daily bread, daily filling, daily sustaining, daily life.

You only have to live today, today, and you never have to live today without God's sustaining power.

You can't do all the hard things. You can't make all the good choices. But you don't have to. You only have to live today, today, and you never have to live today without God's sustaining power.

For Reflection and Discussion

1 What past assumptions of yours might be fueling your grief? What did you expect of the future that's now impossible due to loss? Make a long list. It's important to know exactly what losses you're grieving.

2 How does James's approach to planning for the future make you feel? Consider all the emotions it provokes and try to figure out why you're feeling each of those ways.

3 How might you change the way you live in the present in light of your lack of control over the future? What might you do to actively pursue a loose grip?

4 What can you be certain of in the future? Make a list of things you can know.

5 How might the principle of daily bread affect the way you endure grief? What are you trying to carry today that belongs to tomorrow? What do you need to put down?

Resources

Howe, Marie, and Michael Klein, eds. *In the Comfort of My Solitude: American Writing from the AIDS Pandemic.*

Essays, articles, and reflections from survivors of AIDS, people who grieved loved ones lost to AIDS, and others affected by the disease, this collection includes several helpful glimpses into what it means to live without unhealthy expectations of the future. These stories of grief help us come to terms with our own mortality and the mortality of the people we love.

Gerhardt, JL. *Think Good: How to Get Rid of Anxiety, Fear, Despair and the Like to Finally Find Peace of Mind.*

If in your grief you're struggling with anxiety about the future or fear of further loss, consider this book I wrote, primarily the chapters on living in the future, taking control of our thoughts, and the power of pursuing and entertaining positive, constructive thinking. Grief can do great damage to our ability to regulate our thoughts. Let this be a guide for getting back control.

7

Seeing Clearly: The Gifts of Mortality and Immortality

We have this practice in the Gerhardt home of framing all future plans under the banner of "Lord willing." Lord willing, we'll go on vacation. Lord willing, we'll update the bathroom. Lord willing, we'll celebrate our twentieth anniversary. One time in a sermon on James 4 (the passage of Scripture we considered last chapter) my husband told the church, "You don't have any idea what will happen tomorrow. You might die tomorrow. Jesus might come back tomorrow. Russia might invade Texas tomorrow." The other day my daughter told me what kind of ninth birthday party she wanted. She said, "If Jesus doesn't come back and I don't die and Russia doesn't invade, can I have a circus birthday party?"

Is this strange behavior for an eight-year-old?

When I was eight I talked about death a lot. My grandmother had recently died of cancer. I'd been beside her bed for much of her sickness, drawing pictures to cheer her up. When we pushed her into the mausoleum wall, my whole world changed. It was like suddenly I'd seen backstage and knew the play was an act. Life wasn't what I'd thought; it wasn't sturdy or certain.

After my grandmother died, my teacher asked our third-grade class to write a story for a contest. My friend won with a two-page thriller about a puppy and snow. I turned in eight brooding pages on death. The first line was something like, "I looked into the dark, gaping hole where we'd put my Mammaw's body and felt cold."

EIGHT YEARS old or forty-five or ninety-two, we all change in the shadow light of death. Before we witness death, we see one way. We write stories about puppies and snow. After we witness death, we see another way. We write stories about the dark and the cold. That new way of seeing may seem like a curse; it may become a curse, shrouding our sight in despair. But beside the fire of hope, the darkness and the cold are illuminated and warmed, and our changed sight becomes a gift. Grief forces us into a confrontation with what's real and frees us to live with perspective.

Sometimes though, as we awaken to the world where people don't live forever, it takes our eyes a while to adjust.

As we awaken to the world where people don't live forever, it takes our eyes a while to adjust.

Out of the Blue

Joan Didion writes of her husband's death,

> It was in fact the ordinary nature of everything preceding the event that prevented me from truly believing it had happened, absorbing it, incorporating it, getting past it. . . . Confronted with sudden disaster we all focus on how unremarkable the circumstances were in which the unthinkable occurred, the clear blue sky from which the plane fell, the routine errand that ended on the shoulder with the car in flames, the swings where the children were playing as usual when the rattlesnake struck from the ivy.[1]

It was in fact the ordinary nature of everything preceding the event that prevented me from truly believing it had happened.

Likely your loss was this way, too. On the worst day, the day that changed everything for you, kids still gathered at the bus stop. The mail still came. The day's television programming was entirely unaffected. People grocery shopped and carpooled and shaved. At first, after my brother died and then again after my miscarriages, I looked suspiciously at my loss. *Could it be real?* So many people seemed not to have noticed.

As the days passed and the consequences of death spilled across my life, the grief would begin to feel more real than the things around it. Shopping suddenly seemed empty. Decorating my house. Travel.

Television. It was like this grief existed in an extra dimension, making most everything around it seem flat. The truth of death became undeniable, and the distractions that had once seemed so enjoyable and meaningful, now disintegrated like cotton candy in the rain.

If the first stage of grief is denial, perhaps the second is disorientation. Like a child caught in an undertow, flipped and spun underwater, uncertain which way is up, mourners struggle to right themselves. What was is undone. And what is, is unfamiliar. All of our expectations are upended.

If the first stage of grief is denial, perhaps the second is disorientation.

Rob Bell writes in his book *Drops Like Stars* about this disorientation that comes from suffering. He explains:

> If we went to the ballet and everybody in the audience was wearing snorkels or the musicians were all red-haired banjo players with no teeth or instead of being handed a program we were handed a squirrel, we would immediately begin asking, What is this?
>
> But our real question would be, Where is this? Where do we put this? How do we place it? Because our standard reference points . . . won't be there to guide us.
>
> That's often what happens when we suffer. We had things well planned out. We knew what meant what. We had all of our boxes properly organized and labeled. But all of that was disrupted when we began to suffer.[2]

That's it, right? You thought you understood how things worked and then your brother died or your baby died or your grandfather fell asleep in his chair and didn't wake up, and all of a sudden you realize things:

Life doesn't last forever.

The people you love won't always be with you.

Things that mattered a lot yesterday don't matter so much today.

It's like seeing death up close yanks us out of *The Matrix*, the false reality created and propped up by well-meaning (and not-so-well-meaning) humans, people gathering jobs and wealth and relationships and affirmations, stacking them one on top of another, building a wall to protect themselves from the uncertainty of tomorrow and block out the view of the fog.

It's this lifting of the veil, the revelation of impending death, that inspires the Ecclesiastes writer to spend his days chasing after the meaning of life. He writes, "For who knows what is good for a person in life, during the few and meaningless days they pass through like a shadow? Who can tell them what will happen under the sun after they are gone?" (Eccl 6:12).

Grief upends our understanding of everything, particularly the big things. That might be scary at first, unsettling, unmooring. But, at the same time, it's in and through grief that we get the opportunity to discover (and construct) a new way of seeing (and living) this life. Perhaps the unsettling is a gift; perhaps what we needed most was the perspective we find in the unmooring.

It's in and through grief that we get the opportunity to discover (and construct) a new way of seeing (and living) this life.

Mortality

Martha Whitmore Hickman writes in her book of meditations on grief, "To survive the death of a loved one is no guarantee of greater wisdom. We can also become embittered, reclusive, grasping." She's right; I've seen it happen, watched friends enter the tunnel of grief and never come out. "But," Martha writes, "if we can weather the storm, we will have a better sense of who we are and what we want

> You live as if you were destined to live forever, no thought of your frailty ever enters your head, of how much time has already gone by you take no heed. You squander time as if you drew from a full and abundant supply.
>
> —Seneca, "On the Shortness of Life"[3]

most in life." I've seen that happen, too. Often, the people who are best at living are the people who've seen death up close.

If we can weather the storm, we will have a better sense of who we are and what we want most in life.

In the novel *A Happy Marriage*, by Rafael Yglesias, a husband watches his wife die of cancer. He changes her soiled underwear. He picks out her burial plot. It's a beautiful, exhausting book. As the story unfolds, the narrator alternates between past and present, showing us a picture of who Enrique (the husband) was before the cancer and who he is now, having come to terms with his wife's death. The difference is stark. Sometimes he doesn't see how much he's changed. Sometimes it's all he can see. As Enrique reflects, the narrator observes:

> Her illness had changed something basic in the mechanism of Enrique's head and heart. . . . At long last, after decades of fussing, having watched his father die slowly, and now the mother of his children waste away, he was convinced that death was more than the nearest way to resolve a character's story, that death was, in fact, real. He understood, right into the nucleus of every one of his brain cells, that he and everyone on earth would soon be gone.[4]

It's in this powerful encounter with mortality that Enrique begins the process of reconsidering and rebuilding his life.

Beside a dying body, or a dead one, life looks different.

Shorter.

Beside a dying body, or a dead one, life looks different. Shorter.

The Ecclesiastes writer says you'll find the wise person not in the house of pleasure, but in the house of mourning. He says, "It is better to go to a house of mourning / than to go to a house of feasting / for death is the destiny of everyone; / the living should take this to heart" (7:2–3).

It is better to go to a house of mourning / than to go to a house of feasting.

This is a common refrain in Scripture. Again and again we find God telling humans they're mortal, and encouraging them to embrace their mortality. It starts in the third chapter of the Bible: "For dust you are and to dust you will return" (Gen 3:19). Later, in the Psalms we read,

- "What man can live and not see death?" (89:48).
- "As for man, his days are like grass; / As a flower of the field, so he flourishes. When the wind has passed over it, it is no more, / And its place acknowledges it no longer" (103:15–16).
- "You turn people back to dust, / saying, 'Return to dust, you mortals'" (90:3).

What man can live and not see death?

As we saw last chapter, James writes, "What is your life? You are a mist that appears for a little while and then vanishes" (4:14). And then there's this moving line from an unnamed woman who appears before King David: "For we will surely die and are like water spilled on the ground which cannot be gathered up again" (2 Sam 14:14).

You can skip over those verses when you don't know they're true. But sitting on the ground looking at a tombstone, knowing the person buried beneath it was alive last week, that helps you let it sink in.

The gift of grief is the reminder, you're going to die. Let that reminder change the way you live. Let it inspire you to use the time you have intentionally. Let it stir you to reexamine and reconsider and rebuild your life. Let it move you to action. Let it prompt generosity and kindness. Let it help you love and forgive. Moses writes in Psalm 90, "Teach us to number our days, / That we may present to you a heart of wisdom" (90:12). Number your days and let that number, finite and ever-shrinking, make you wise.

The gift of grief is the reminder, you're going to die.

Immortality

The first time I learned about perspective in elementary school art class, my teacher explained how to draw a road. The lines shouldn't stay equal distance apart on the page, but they should angle toward one another, even appear to meet on the horizon. He showed us pictures of roads, and we looked at the lanes growing smaller and smaller, knowing in our heads that the lane two miles down the road was exactly as wide as the lane at the forefront of the image. If I'd only ever seen a picture of a road from eye level, I might assume all roads eventually end, shrinking in on themselves until they disappear. But because I've traveled roads, and because I've seen roads from above, I know what appears to be an end is actually just more road.

What appears to be an end is actually just more road.

When my husband preaches funerals he often quotes *Peter Pan*, that famous line about death as "an awfully big adventure." He says those words from behind a podium, usually just above the coffin. Sometimes the casket is open when he says them, and when it is I have a harder time believing him. *Death as adventure, huh?*

Death is undeniably an end. The body in the coffin, stiff and lifeless, serves as proof. But death is also not *the* end. In some ways it's more like a beginning.

- That seems to be the message of Scripture:
- Jesus says "I am the resurrection and the life; he who believes in me will live even if he dies, and everyone who lives and believes in me will never die. Do you believe this?" (John 11:25–26).
- Isaiah says, "He will swallow up death for all time, and the Lord God will wipe tears away from all faces" (25:8).
- Paul says Jesus "has destroyed death and has brought life and immortality to light" (1 Tim 1:10).
- Jesus tells the Sadducees who deny the resurrection, "He is not the God of the dead, but of the living. You are badly mistaken!" (Mark 12:27).

I am the resurrection and the life; he who believes in me will live even if he dies, and everyone who lives and believes in me will never die. Do you believe this?

We said earlier that the gift of grief is the reminder of our own mortality. That's true. We're all dying. But we could also say, the gift of grief is the reminder of our immortality, of the eternal life to come. In grief, we come face to face not just with death, but also with the hope of resurrection and eternal life.

The gift of grief is the reminder of our immortality, of the eternal life to come.

- David writes in Psalm 16:11, "You make known to me the path of life; you will fill me with joy in your presence, with eternal pleasures at your right hand."

- Jesus says to Nicodemus, "For God so loved the world that he gave his one and only Son, that whoever believes in him shall not perish but have eternal life" (John 3:16).
- Jesus says to the Samaritan woman, "But whoever drinks the water I give them will never thirst. Indeed, the water I give them will become in them a spring of water welling up to eternal life" (John 4:14).
- In Romans chapter 5, Paul affirms the pursuit of immortality as holy. He says, "To those who by persistence in doing good seek glory, honor and immortality, he will give eternal life" (v. 21).
- He'll later write to Timothy, "Fight the good fight of the faith. Take hold of the eternal life to which you were called" (1 Tim 6:12).
- In his letters to the early church, the apostle John writes, "And this is what he promised us—eternal life."

Indeed, the water I give them will become in them a spring of water welling up to eternal life.

The headline promise in the kingdom of God is that in Christ we'll live forever; that promise changes the way we face death. It makes us brave. And that promise changes the way we face life. It makes us bold.

I heard author and speaker Christine Caine say once that Christians should all be "a little bit naughty." What she meant was that we should walk around with a kind of defiant confidence, a delightful boldness that surprises and intrigues. When I'm feeling especially empowered by my inheritance of eternal life, I'll say with the Hebrews writer, "What can mere mortals do to me?" (13:6).

Grief is an opportunity to finally, fully buy in to the hope of resurrection and to let that hope make you bold.

Grief is an opportunity to finally, fully buy in to the hope of resurrection and to let that hope make you bold.

One night after my brother died, I dreamed that I saw him. It was one dream in a series of dreams I'd been having in which Bobby showed up at family functions. In these scenarios I would be the only person who realized Bobby had died and been brought back. I hugged him like a pencil topper, refusing to let go.

In what would turn out to be the last dream about my brother I'd ever have, Bobby, exhausted by my fawning (though still kind and gentle), said, "Jen, it's going to be okay. Jesus is coming back in four . . ." And then suddenly, the word *four* still on his lips, my brother's eyebrows shot up, his mouth went tight, and he disappeared.

End of dream.

As soon I woke up I was certain, God himself had snatched Bobby out of my dream for spilling the beans about the approaching resurrection date. I wrote down the date the next morning. Just in case.

Jesus didn't show up four days later. He didn't show up four months later, and he didn't show up four years later either. Lately I'm convinced Bobby was about to say four hundred years. But maybe I'm wrong. Maybe God isn't in the habit of handing out top-secret information to new guys.

Grief has opened my heart to the promise of immortality, and grief has enabled the promise of immortality to shape my heart.

For me, the idea of a resurrection day, of a time when Christ will return and raise the dead to life and gather the living, isn't some unicorns-and-fairies dream. I'm counting on it. I'm making plans to see my brother and my grandmother, my grandfather, maybe even my babies. I'm betting everything on it. Paul says, "If only for this life we have hope in Christ, we are of all people most to be pitied." It's true. If there's no life after death, I've made some very stupid choices.

Grief has opened my heart to the promise of immortality, and grief has enabled the promise of immortality to shape my heart.

Vantage Points

A couple years ago my husband and I hiked two extraordinary trails in Zion National Park in Utah, Angel's Landing and The Narrows. Angel's Landing is a 1,500-foot climb with 1,000-foot drop-offs. I sat on a rock near the summit and ate lunch with my husband and friends, peering out over a lush valley, red rock mountains, and a winding river; I felt like I'd climbed into the clouds to have lunch with God. The next day we hiked The Narrows, a hike through a riverbed at the bottom of a canyon, vertical sandstone cliffs shooting up all around us to heights of as much as 2,400 feet. I couldn't stop thinking of how different everything looked from down here. Twenty-four hours before I'd been a giant, looking down on boulders like pebbles and rivers like ribbons. Now I was an ant, a speck, looking up, feeling so far from the clouds. Taken together, the two views offered a fuller, truer sense of what was.

Here are two things we learn in grief:

1. Life is short. Be wise.

2. Life is long. Be bold.

Here are two things we learn in grief:

Life is short. Be wise.

Life is long. Be bold.

Taken together, these two truths offer a fuller, truer sense of how to live a life.

I don't know how to read the book of Revelation, not exactly. But I do know John's vision of a new kingdom and a new earth in which God is making everything new is a vision for people who're suffering and a vision for people who're waiting.

As John's revelation closes, the angel shows him one last view. John stands like a tourist at a scenic overlook and sees the river of life "as clear as crystal, flowing from the throne of God and of the Lamb down the middle of the great street of the city." "On each side of the river" he sees the tree of life, "bearing twelve crops of fruit, yielding its fruit every month." Later in this passage John will note the complete absence of night: "They will not need the light of a lamp or the light of the sun, for the Lord God will give them light" (22:1–5).

John experiences a reorientation here. His eyes are opened, and he observes reality from a brand-new position. When he sees what God has for him to see, he notices that in the kingdom of God, time isn't the same. It's not measured by nights and days, the rising and

> Your days are numbered. Use them to throw open the windows of your soul to the sun. If you do not, the sun will soon set, and you with it.
>
> —Marcus Aurelius, *The Emperor's Handbook*[5]

setting of a sun. Life in the kingdom is defined by a constant and abiding light. It's not measured by planting season or growing season or harvest. There's no winter or fall. Just month after month after month of fruit.

Standing beside John, looking at that tree of life and then at my own fruitless limbs, heavy with sorrow, empty of light, weighed down with winter, I have perspective. I see two truths, far apart but drawing closer as they edge toward the horizon.

For Reflection and Discussion

1. Do you feel disoriented by grief? How so? What's been upended in your life?
2. How have you reacted to the realization that life doesn't last forever? Is that easy or hard for you to get your head around? How does it make you feel?
3. Do you think grief is making you a different person? If so, how so?
4. How does hope shape the way you respond to death—the deaths of others and the inevitability of your own death?
5. Do you feel like grief has given you perspective? How do you see differently?
6. How did this sentence make you feel: "Christians live an expansive, ever-multiplying and unfolding, eternal life"? Is it true? If it were true, what would that mean? How might it change the way we grieve?

Resources

Hickman, Martha Whitmore. *Healing after Loss: Daily Meditations for Working Through Grief.*

Hickman's collection of short meditations for the grieving is thoughtful, compact, and helpful. The quotes she's tracked down aren't bumper sticker platitudes, but rather thoughtful excerpts from good books, poems, and resources written by wise people.

Yglesias, Rafael. *A Happy Marriage.*

A visceral, moving, raw, sometimes graphic depiction of a marriage in which the main character cares for his wife as she dies. Largely, he reflects on the nature of their relationship and who he'll be when she's gone. There's great writing here. This book is particularly powerful for those mourning a spouse, but any married person who's experienced suffering can relate.

Hislop, Victoria, ed. *Loss.*

This compilation of stories about grief is entirely composed by female writers. Each one prods, pokes, or comforts. The two I find most instructive in loss are "The Merry Widow" by Margaret Drabble and "Father, Father" by Susan Hill. Each story represents an entirely different way of handling grief, but both deal with disorientation and rebuilding.

8

Remembering: The Gift of Inspiration

Roger lost his wife, Carolyn, to cancer after forty years of marriage, just after the birth of their first grandchild, just before the retirement they'd been so eager to enjoy. He lives in a small town where pretty much everybody knows everybody, so everybody knows Carolyn died—people in the grocery store, people at church, people at the post office. Roger messaged me a while back because he'd heard I was writing a book about grief and had something he wanted to say. Tired of what seemed like a wall of awkward silence encircling him, Roger wished people would speak freely, wished they'd treat him the same way they did before the loss. He wrote, "Honestly, sometimes in the church building people turn and talk to someone else so they don't have to face me. I don't think I'm imagining that. It's happened too many times."

Roger, full of grace, said he figured people "don't know what to say." Should they talk about his wife? Should they not? Most of the time they don't. And that makes Roger sad. He wrote,

> I try my best to keep Carolyn's memory alive. I talk about her all the time in the flow of conversation. Not to the point of being overboard, but you don't just toss forty years of someone. . . . People need to understand that it's not only okay to talk with a person who is going through major grief about the loved one they lost, it's okay for them to tell you how much they miss the person too.

IN MOST cases, it's more than okay. Sometimes it's the thing the griever needs most.

If you've never lost someone close, it makes sense that you'd be tongue-tied in the presence of unfamiliar pain. It takes a certain kind of wisdom to know just how much a grieving person wants to talk about their loved one. It takes bravery and empathy to bear the potential of another person's tears. But if you're a person who has grieved, you know what a gift it can be to sit across a table and listen to someone talk about your person.

It's not only okay to talk with a person who is going through major grief about the loved one they lost, it's okay for them to tell you how much they miss the person too.

A year or so ago I received an email from a guy I don't know. He's married with a kid, has a job, seems upstanding and nice. He told me he'd wanted to send this email for a while, but just now had gotten up the nerve. He worried it would make me sad. He said he wanted to tell me a story about my brother.

> Sharing tales of those we've lost is how we keep from really losing them.
>
> —Mitch Albom, *For One More Day*[1]

One day when this guy was a high schooler visiting colleges, trying to decide where he'd go, he ended up in Bobby's dorm room. In his story, Bobby—generous, fun, and kind—ends up giving him a pair of his shoes. He describes them, and I remember the first time I saw Bobby wearing them, black-and-white Doc Martens, flashy and expensive. This guy said that now, fourteen years later, he still remembers my brother's kindness, says when he was in college he shared a pair of shoes with a high schooler himself.

I've never heard the story before, but it seems right, like certainly this is the way things would have gone down. I read the details over and over. That's Bobby. Those are his shoes. This email makes me laugh and cry, and for a minute it resurrects my brother from the dead.

Now that he *is* dead, I will never make a new memory with him. My supply is limited to what I've already collected, memories I've gone over again and again like tired photographs carried to war, pulled in and out of dirty pockets. That's why other people's memories are so special. They're new, not at all faded, crisp and clear, an opportunity to see my person again through fresh eyes.

Most of the mourners I've met are like Roger and me; we do want to talk about our person. We want to tell stories and hear stories and remember. There's power in remembering, particularly remembering out loud in community. It reminds us that the life we lived before was real and true and not an elaborate dream. And it confirms for us the truth that our person hasn't disappeared.

There's power in remembering, particularly remembering out loud in community. It reminds us that the life we lived before was real and true and not an elaborate dream. And it confirms for us the truth that our person hasn't disappeared.

Séance

Bobby had been dead for about six hours the first time I talked about him in the past tense. In those six hours, I'd managed to pack a bag, call some of his closest friends, and buy plane tickets. In the car on the way to the airport I asked my husband to stop at Chick-fil-A for a sandwich. I said, "Bobby loved Chick-fil-A." I caught the tense shift the minute I spoke it. When the lady handed me my sandwich at the drive-through window, I refused to eat it. I'd tainted it by relegating my brother to the past.

For a few days that's how I felt about Bobby, like he lived in the past now, like he'd moved to a time and place I couldn't visit. But then some friends of his and I went out to the beach after his viewing to tell stories. We sat on familiar sand, listening to the familiar soundtrack of waves and gulls, sounds we'd shared with Bobby for twenty years. We sat together, a group of people connected only by our shared love of Bobby, and we told stories about how Bobby had salted his ketchup, how he'd known all the custodians at our college by name, how he'd pretended to try out for *American Idol* in the shower and lost. Every word we spoke resurrected some part of my brother, one part after another, until eventually, close to midnight, under one street light and a billion stars, Bobby had been brought back to life.

Ever since then my husband and I have done our best to talk about Bobby as if he's still alive, because we believe he is. He's alive literally, waiting in sleep for the great resurrection. And he's alive figuratively, his legacy all around us, kept alive by the stories we tell, the memories we faithfully dust off and display. I say, "I have a brother," and embrace the awkward conversations to come when people inevitably ask where he lives.

What are some of your favorite memories of your loved one? Take a few minutes and write about one memory that means a lot to you. You might consider keeping a journal and writing one new memory each day.

About four years ago both my grandfathers died within two weeks of one another. My husband preached one funeral, and I preached the other. Within my family's faith tradition, women don't preach, so I wasn't a candidate for my mother's father's funeral. Justin was, and he did an excellent job. But my second grandfather to die wasn't a Christian, and his funeral wasn't so much worship as remembrance, so no one minded me being the one to direct our thoughts. At my first grandfather's funeral, Justin talked a lot about heaven, resurrection, and reunion, about how this wasn't the end. At my second grandfather's funeral, we didn't talk about that.

I don't believe I'll see him again. I understand not everyone would agree with me on that. I'd be delighted to find out I'm wrong. I believe resurrection comes to those who've committed to follow Christ, and I worried for years about how I'd handle the eventual death of my grandparents who had, in word and practice, committed *not* to follow Christ.

When it came time to preach his funeral, all the worries were gone. I knew just what to say: Poppa was a beautiful man, a kind grandfather, and a generous friend. He built award-winning racecars and optimized the system for ordering parts at his General Electric plant. He corresponded with people all across the world, laboriously tracing our family history all the way back to John Smith and Pocahontas. He sent a letter telling the coach of the professional soccer team in town what changes to make on the roster (and received a letter of thanks back). These are the stories I told at his funeral, stories of a man with a keen eye for how things work and how to make things work better, a man who loved his grandkids and great grandkids, a man who worked hard and never met a stranger. As I told these stories Poppa seemed to rise in our midst. Also, I began to see Poppa's legacy deeply ingrained in the people gathered in the pews. I saw Poppa's face in my dad's, the same weathered skin, the same creases across his forehead. I saw Poppa's eye for perennial improvement in me, ever tinkering with everything, unable to overlook a problem. I saw Poppa in my daughter Eve, making friends on playgrounds across the country, a list of children's names and phone numbers saved on my phone. Looking around the room, I realized Poppa was here.

The act of remembering does more than help us look back at what was; it reminds us of what is, what lingers of the person we loved. Remembering my loved ones reminds me that they're not gone. They're here, among us. And so many of them are there ahead of us, too.

The act of remembering does more than help us look back at what was; it reminds us of what is, what lingers of the person we loved.

Remembering my loved ones reminds me that they're not gone. They're here, among us. And so many of them are there ahead of us, too.

I can't help but think of Hebrews chapter 11 and the long list of people described by God as examples of faith, our spiritual ancestors living among us in legacy. The Hebrews writer looks back on this extraordinary crew of people and says, "Therefore, since we are surrounded by such a great cloud of witnesses, let us throw off everything that hinders and the sin that so easily entangles. And let us run with perseverance the race marked out for us" (Heb 12:1). Are these men and women literally looking down and cheering us on? Not exactly. It's more like their testimonies, the powerful lives they lived, surround us, uphold us, and inspire us. Every time we tell a story about Abraham or Daniel or Rahab we summon them from the grave. Every time we follow their example, we carry on their legacy; their faith lives on in us.

Unstuck

One of the great temptations in grief is the tendency to live in the past, to focus more on what happened than on what's happening now. Instead of inviting our loved one's memory and legacy into our present life, we'll avoid our present life by holding too tightly to the memory of how things used to be.

In recent years I've seen Facebook's "memories" feature hold people hostage this way, calling them back again and again to a life they no longer live with pictures and posts at the top of their news feed. A friend of mine told me, "Every time I see one of those pictures or read my words from before he died, it's like a punch in the gut." And yet, this friend hasn't turned off the feature. She's stuck in an eddy of melancholy reminiscing. Instead of posting about her current adventures, routines, frustrations, or joys, she's locked into obsessing over the life she can't stop missing. When that happens to us, we find our memories hog-tying our chance at building a new life.

In the book of Deuteronomy in the Hebrew Scriptures, God prepares his people for a journey into the promised land. Through Moses, God inspires the Israelites to look ahead to the future with confidence and faith. It's this future orientation that makes one repeated phrase stick out. Over and over in Deuteronomy, we find the word *remember*, most often as a command to remember the good things God did in the past. Moses says,

- Remember that you were slaves in Egypt and that the Lord your God brought you out of there with a mighty hand and an outstretched arm (Deut 5:15).
- But do not be afraid of them; remember well what the Lord your God did to Pharaoh and to all Egypt (Deut 7:18).
- Remember how the Lord your God led you all the way in the wilderness these forty years (Deut 8:2).
- Remember that you were slaves in Egypt and the Lord your God redeemed you (Deut 15:15).
- Remember that you were slaves in Egypt and the Lord your God redeemed you from there (Deut 24:18).
- Remember the days of old; / consider the generations long past. / Ask your father and he will tell you, / your elders, and they will explain to you. / When the Most High gave the nations their inheritance . . . (Deut 32:7–8).

Remember how the Lord your God led you all the way.

God encourages his people to remember the past in order to walk with assurance into the future.

Our remembering shouldn't wreck us in the past, stranding us on the rocks of moments we'll never have again. Instead, those memories have the potential to remind us of what's possible with God.

In each case, God encourages his people to remember the past in order to walk with assurance into the future.

What does this have to do with grief? Too often, when we do embrace the gift of remembering, we struggle with the weight of those beautiful memories, memories made smooth and shiny over time as they fade in the precision and grittiness of truth. We remember joy in the past and feel more acutely our lack in the present. We remember the good old days and think nothing could ever be that good again. I wonder if Israel had that same nagging suspicion. I wonder if they reminisced about the good old days when God parted seas and doled out deliverance through plagues, afraid those days were over. If they did, God certainly corrected them.

The point of remembering in Deuteronomy is this: If God could do that then, imagine what God could do now. The point of remembering in grief is partly the same. Our remembering shouldn't wreck us in the past, stranding us on the rocks of moments we'll never have again. Instead, those memories have the potential to remind us of what's possible with God, to reawaken us to the potential for blessing and connection and joy. If things were good then, they can surely be good again. How can we be certain? Because every good gift comes from above. And the blessings he once gave testify to the certainty of the blessings he'll give tomorrow.

As you remember your loved one, let their memory be an inspiration for you to live a full and faith-filled life. See the person you were blessed to love and live alongside as proof of God's grace. If he gave you that gift in the past, imagine what he might have in store for your future.

Made Resilient

My daughter Eve is my brother Bobby reincarnated; full of life and mischief, wit and kindness, she connects with every person she

How to help friends and loved ones share their memories:

1 Ask people to share their memories with you in letters, emails, or short videos. Use social media both to request stories and to share them.

2 Invite people over for a night of storytelling. Give prompts:

- Tell about a time when ________ made you laugh, made you late, made you angry, made you think.
- Talk about a time when you and ________ shared an especially good meal, a scary adventure, a heartfelt talk.
- Describe ________________ in three words.
- What Disney princess was ________________ most like and why?
- How did ________________ inspire you?
- What will you miss most about ________________?

3 Don't expect people to always want to talk about your loved one. Remember that not everyone finds joy in remembering, and most people can only handle so much melancholy.

4 If someone mentions your loved one in conversation and then seems uncomfortable, quickly share how glad you are that they felt comfortable talking about him or her. Say, "I love hearing her name. It brings back good memories." If it does make you uncomfortable, say that too. But don't overreact. You may feel differently later.

meets. We tell her she's his twin, and she grins. Often we'll be riding in the truck, and Eve will yell up to the front seat, "Mom, tell me a story about Uncle Bert." That's what she calls him, Uncle Bert. It melts my heart.

From the day they were born, my girls have heard stories about their uncle. At age two London would walk around the house holding his picture, telling him about her day. Though he's not here to hold them or jump on the trampoline with them or teach them to play basketball, I'm resolved to make sure they grow up knowing him and learning from who he was while he was here. In a very real way, my girls will grow up with their uncle. They'll grow up with his memory and legacy. One day they'll meet him and recognize him from the stories.

> The life of the dead is placed in the memory of the living.
>
> —Marcus Tullius Cicero, "The 14 Orations Against Marcus Antonius" (Oration 9, part V)[2]

I wonder sometimes if my brother had lived, what my girls might have thought of him. I wonder if I'd have spoken of him so fondly. I wonder if I'd have remembered so many good moments from childhood. In our grief, we find ourselves compelled to remember our loved ones. We make slide shows of pictures. We gather after the funeral to tell embarrassing stories. We send letters expressing our best memories of the person who died. It's funny how sometimes it takes a death to recall how much we loved a person. Sometimes death is the key to remembering, and remembering, though not as good as experiencing, is an extraordinary gift.

> Sometimes death is the key to remembering, and remembering, though not as good as experiencing, is an extraordinary gift.

Recently I read an article in the *New York Times* by Bruce Feiler on what makes happy families and successful kids. Feiler says, "The single most important thing you can do for your family may be the simplest of all: develop a strong family narrative." Citing psychologist Marshall Duke's thorough research with children enduring stress he says, "The more children knew about their family's history, the stronger their sense of control over their lives, the higher their self-esteem and the more successfully they believed their families functioned." Dr. Duke connected self-confidence in children with what he called a strong "intergenerational self." In other words, "They know they belong to something bigger than themselves."[3]

That's what remembering does for a person. It positions the present in the context of the past. It allows our relatives and friends, dead and gone, a seat at the family table, speaking wisdom from then to empower us now. Remembering tethers us to something bigger.

> Remembering tethers us to something bigger.

For Reflection and Discussion

1. Do people avoid talking to you about your loved one? If so, how does that make you feel?
2. Have you made remembering an intentional practice? What might it look like to practice remembering every day?

3 Do you have a community in which you can remember your person? Who might you reach out to in order to share memories more intentionally?

4 Have you become mired in the past? Do you ever get caught up in remembering and let that reminiscence pull you down into melancholy and despair? How might you reframe your memories in order to help you in your present life? What memories of your loved one inspire you to live fully today?

Resources

Feiler, Bruce. *The Secrets of Happy Families.*

This is the book into which Feiler incorporates his research on families and storytelling. If you're interested in a longer look at how intentional remembering can help strengthen your family, this is a helpful resource.

Coco, from Disney Pixar.

I took my kids to see this movie and wept through the last twenty minutes. While I don't love what I perceive to be the idolization of family, I do think the story gets at the heart of what we're communicating in this chapter. Remembering our loved ones is one way we keep them alive, and it's the only way we're able to continue learning from their wisdom.

Mitchell, Patricia. "Remember!" https://tinyurl.com/y8kqf4cu.

In this practical article from *Christianity Today*, Mitchell explains the use of an Ebenezer stone in the Old Testament and guides you through an exercise to develop a similar but personalized reminder of God's past faithfulness to rely upon in present trouble.

9

Reaching Out: The Gift of Comfort

I was teaching Tolstoy when it happened, Tolstoy or Chekhov, one or the other, some Russian writer living in the snow, writing about death and despair. I was teaching Tolstoy to teenagers and twenty-somethings living in Alabama in the twenty-first century and feeling like maybe they didn't understand this kind of pain. Before I could stop myself I was telling them about the car accident, about Bobby hitting the tree, about what it's like to grieve a loss, so tragic and meaningless. I hoped this would help them understand Tolstoy. And life.

After class one of my students came up to the lectern. I saw him headed my way and grabbed the class roll, trying to remember his name. His long blond hair covered half his pale face. He lifted his hand, pushed his hair aside, and said, out of nowhere, "My dad died in a car accident around the same time as your brother. Can I ask you, how is it that you seem like you're doing okay?"

That was the first sentence I'd ever heard Matt Cross speak, Matt who would become my second brother. In the months to follow he and I and my husband would eat Mexican food together every Sunday, we'd play cards together, we'd have long, serious talks together, and eventually my husband Justin would baptize Matt in the cold Flint River. My daughters would be the flower girls in his wedding. This summer we'll meet up to share a bottle of red wine from 2002, the year his dad and my brother died, the year our fates became entwined.

If you ask me what brought us together, why, after all these years, we're friends, the answer would be undeniable: grief. Matt and I don't have much in common beyond our losses. Matt grew up in a small town in the South. I grew up in urban, coastal Florida. Matt likes metal bands. I sing along to a cappella hymns in my car. Matt was a student. I was his teacher. We weren't alike. But from the moment Matt shared his story, telling me about driving to school and pulling up on his dad's accident, I knew we would be bound to one another for a long, long time. There's something about shared suffering that stitches souls together.

There's something about shared suffering that stitches souls together.

AFTER MY brother died I felt distant from people to whom I'd once felt close. Conversations seemed shallow, games seemed silly, outings seemed frivolous. I felt like no one could understand my pain, and thus no one could understand me in this season defined by pain. My friend Roxanne felt the same thing when her mother died, like no one understood and no one could relate. She said, "No one can remotely understand how you feel unless they have somewhat walked in your shoes." My friend Brooke, after losing a father figure in her life wrote, "I didn't really have any close friends who had experienced the loss of a parent when I was going through Ron's illness and death. So I felt very alone because my friends, while caring, just didn't understand."

Not only did I feel like my friends didn't understand, I also noticed their distinct lack of comfort around me. People didn't know what to say or how to act. Looking back, I'm thankful they tried, but in the moment, their discomfort only cemented the distance between us.

> Friendship . . . is born at the moment when one man says to another "What! You too? I thought that no one but myself . . ."
>
> —C. S. Lewis,
> *The Four Loves*[1]

In my grief I felt lonely. Most people do. At the same time, though, perhaps because of my loneliness and hunger for understanding, I felt compelled to connect with others who might have felt the same pain. I started with books, weeping through C. S. Lewis's *A Grief Observed* and Joan Didion's *The Year of Magical Thinking*. I read their stories and understood my story better. Later, when I was more emotionally stable and less averse to being vulnerable, I reached out to acquaintances and people at church, looking for fellow sufferers, anyone who might have felt this pain before, anyone to help me walk the path they'd walked already.

Suffering connects the sufferers.

In his book *Drops Like Stars*, Rob Bell asks his reader to imagine being at a public event like a movie or game or play or religious service. Before it starts, someone says to the crowd, "Please stand if you've been affected by cancer."[2] He notes how powerful a moment like this can be, how connected the people standing feel to one another, and then wonders aloud, "If someone said, 'Please stand . . . if you've been to Hawaii' or 'Please stand . . . if you've had to fire your interior decorator' or 'Please stand . . . if you drive a station wagon,' it just wouldn't have the same effect, would it?"[3]

Of course it wouldn't. All commonalities do bind, but some are weak ties. It's interesting that we both drive the same kind of car, but that's not enough to make us friends. Suffering, though, suffering is strong. Bell writes,

> It doesn't matter if you're rich or poor or black or white or right or left or young or old—if you have the same disease as someone else or if you both have a daughter with an eating disorder or have a brother in jail or have a spouse die or recently were fired . . . you have a bond that transcends whatever differences you have. That's what suffering does.[4]

In a season when we're feeling especially alone, grief offers the gift of community and connection.

Suffering connects the sufferers.

In a season when we're feeling especially alone, grief offers the gift of community and connection.

Hurdles

I have no natural aptitude when it comes to community. I like to be alone. I feel weird in groups. I say awkward things. I never ask the right questions at parties. In my efforts to figure this community thing out, and not live as a hermit, I've paid attention to the skills required for connection. Two of them stick out as absolutely essential if we intend to find comfort and connection in grief:

1. You have to be willing to be vulnerable.

2. You have to be willing to listen.

These aren't easy postures to maintain under normal circumstances. In grief, they're harder.

After a loss we tend to hedge our relational bets, afraid of losing another person. That might look like refusing to make new friends (What if they leave?) or refusing to be vulnerable (What if I'm injured?). Mourners seek safety. Understandable, but all that hunkering down has the negative effect of isolating us, which is good for no one and ultimately dangerous.

Fortunately, people who've suffered, particularly people of hope, are often some of the safest people around. They're the most likely to understand your pain, respect it, and respond with empathy. My friend Erin told me, "I feel safer with these people [people who've suffered]. I feel like they can handle 'big' things without having major reactions. They can more easily absorb shock, grief, fear, anxiety, and get on to being helpful, caring, or generally unshakeable." My husband said, after Bobby died it was like he now had "access to another dimension of human experience." Being around others who'd experienced something similar felt like being around people who spoke the same second language, people who'd spent time in the same far-off places you had. You both knew the world was bigger. You both had a grounding perspective. You could feel comfortable with a fellow sufferer.

It's not just our desire for safety that stands in the way of connection. It can also be our pride. Certain that our own grief is so unique no one could ever understand, we close ourselves off to what could be beautiful, encouraging friendships.

At first, that's how I felt. I had a half-dozen people reach out to me after Bobby died, a guy from church whose sister died by suicide, a

Mourners seek safety… Fortunately, people who've suffered, particularly people of hope, are often some of the safest people around. They're the most likely to understand your pain, respect it, and respond with empathy.

It's not just our desire for safety that stands in the way of connection. It can also be our pride.

friend from college whose sister had died in a car wreck, a woman who'd lost her daughter in a tragic accident. In every case, I found a reason to push those people away:

- My brother didn't die by suicide; you couldn't understand.
- I was so close to my brother, and you weren't as close to your sister; you couldn't understand.
- My brother was young, and your daughter was middle-aged; you don't understand.

My thinking was, if no one grieves the same way and no one's been through the exact circumstances I have, how could anyone have anything valuable to share with me? I fixated on the differences between our situations instead of focusing on the similarity. I decided no one else could understand my unique and terrible pain. And I was wrong.

I decided no one else could understand my unique and terrible pain. And I was wrong.

I have a friend, Kim, who lost her brother, sister-in-law, and two nieces in a car accident. After the accident she immediately took over as guardian for her nephew, the lone survivor of the head-on crash caused by a drunk driver. I've talked to her numerous times about grief, about hers and mine and grief in general, and you know what's most refreshing about those conversations? Her marked humility. Not only does Kim not feel like her grief is more special than other people's grief, she's generous when she listens to others talk about theirs. Empathetic and never condescending, Kim recognizes that all pain is painful, and all pain is more bearable shared.

All pain is painful, and all pain is more bearable shared.

Yes, grief is unique. Yes, every circumstance does lead down a different road of endurance and healing. But it is undeniably true that loss is common, and that almost every loss has about it the same feelings, pains, and hurdles. If we desire connection, we'll find it (despite differences in our stories). And if we're humble enough to receive whatever wisdom and love another sufferer passes along, we'll be better for it.

Circle of Comfort

The apostle Paul opens up his second letter to the Corinthians with praise to "the Father of compassion and the God of all comfort, who comforts us in all our troubles" (v. 3). This is clearly both praise and instruction, words Paul directs to God but says in the presence of others so they might overhear and learn where to turn in trouble. Paul, always wading in suffering, teaches us that God is the ultimate source of comfort and compassion. Paul knows and proclaims a God who sees his people, has compassion, and reaches down to help.

God is the ultimate source of comfort and compassion.

Paul affirms God as comforter, but then goes further to explain how the comfort comes. He writes, "who comforts us in all our troubles so that we can comfort those in any trouble with the comfort we ourselves receive from God." Over the next several verses, Paul describes a pipeline of suffering and comfort, beginning with Christ and flowing through God's people. Paul says that in his suffering he's received comfort from the suffering of Christ, and the purpose of that comfort (perhaps even the purpose of the suffering) is what he's now able to offer others experiencing suffering of their own: comfort. If that sounds a little circular, good. That's the idea.

When we suffer, we find comfort from those who've suffered before and received the comfort of Christ. And, when others suffer, we share our comfort with them. No one is alone in her pain, isolated from God's compassion. Instead, we pass it on, a never-ending circuit of connection and comfort. That is, if everyone does her part.

When we suffer, we find comfort from those who've suffered before and received the comfort of Christ. And, when others suffer, we share our comfort with them.

Paul makes it clear here, there is comfort available for the suffering, and that comfort comes from others who've received it before us. Receiving that comfort looks like receiving the wisdom and experience of others. It looks like asking a friend, "How did you ever survive this?" It looks like sending a Facebook message, starting off, "You don't know me well, but I have some questions for you." It looks like attending a grief support group and welcoming the wisdom you encounter.

My friend Linda participated in a grief support group years ago, and now facilitates a group with her husband. Linda isn't shackled by grief herself anymore. She's received comfort, primarily through this group. Now she tries to extend that comfort as a mentor and friend. She recently shared with me some things people have said about their experience in this kind of community of brokenness and healing:

- At group I found the permission I needed to let grief happen.
- I learned that I'm not alone.
- I discovered I'm not crazy.
- I felt so safe and loved.

Linda can't stop talking about this circle of comfort, about the joy and freedom people find in connection.

Linda is a perfect example of the way comfort works in Christ. She suffered, she found comfort from others who'd suffered before, and after her suffering she sought out other sufferers in order to share the comfort she'd received. While grief never does end exactly, some of us find ourselves further down the road than others. Some of us, in our grief, have found gifts like perspective and belonging. If that's you, God has plans for what you've learned.

Some of us, in our grief, have found gifts like perspective and belonging. If that's you, God has plans for what you've learned.

My friend Brooke told me recently about grieving, "I have found that I am a go-to person for others going through loss." She said about her own grief and the purpose she's found in it, "I was so hurt by some friends who I didn't feel were there for me, that I've been committed to being the person I wished I would have had at that time."

Comforting others can take many forms. Maybe you'll be the person who brings toilet paper, paper plates, and forks to the griever's house. Maybe you'll attend the funeral, knowing how much people in the seats matter. Maybe you'll write a letter of encouragement. Maybe you'll offer your strength in prayer. Maybe you'll babysit the kids. Maybe you'll check in a few weeks or months down the road when the dust clears and fewer people are

Comforting others can take many forms.

clamoring to help. If you don't know how to help, just think back to ways you've been helped. Let the comfort poured out on you pour out on the grieving around you.

The Best Worst Club

I'd spent the day climbing a mountain and exploring the ruins of a medieval castle with my husband and kids. My youngest hopped between giant stones and danced in small rooms carved out of rock. My eldest peered through the tall, thin arrow slits at the small village below and made friends with the butterflies alighting on wildflowers sprung up within the crumbling castle walls. This castle had survived for more than seven hundred years. History and the elements had not been kind, but the construction was solid, and so it endured, in part. We took our picture, all four of us, amid the rubble.

I climbed into bed at a friend's house, tired and happy, opening my laptop for one last look at my emails and Facebook messages. That's when I saw it. An acquaintance from college had lost her brother in a motorcycle accident. I hadn't known her well. She'd known my brother well, though. And tonight she'd messaged me, looking for something. I'm not sure she knew what. She wrote: "I know you are

If you don't know how to help, just think back to ways you've been helped. Let the comfort poured out on you pour out on the grieving around you.

Dos and Don'ts for helping grieving friends

1 Do respond quickly with compassion and comfort.

2 Don't expect them to know what they need (offer what you think they might).

3 Do communicate hope (without being dismissive of their pain).

4 Don't dump your pain on top of theirs (they can't bear their own grief right now).

5 Do tell the truth (vulnerability enables connection).

6 Don't offer advice right away.

7 Do offer advice later.

> As servants of God we commend ourselves in every way: in great endurance; in troubles, hardships and distresses . . . in purity, understanding, patience and kindness; in the Holy Spirit and in sincere love; in truthful speech and in the power of God.
>
> —2 Corinthians 6:4–7

off in Croatia . . . but when you have a moment, I could use some encouragement on how to handle such pain. Where do you go from here?"

All the joy of the day drained from my face, and I cried on my keyboard. What do you say when the worst thing happens? Why message me?

I told my husband what had happened, prayed, and started typing, trying to put my sadness aside for just long enough to assemble some modicum of wisdom. It had been ten years since my brother died, a decade of healing and endurance, and still the pain shot through my nerves and muscles, hot and heavy. I said all I knew to say, hit send, and fell back on the bed, exhausted, still crying. In time she wrote back, "Thank you! Seriously. That is just what I needed. Someone who understands." And though I was shaken, hurting, and emptied, I was glad to have had something to give.

We'd message one another a few more times over the years. Later another friend from college would lose her sister suddenly, and the three of us would form a sort of club. We call it the worst club ever. The dues aren't worth the perks. None of us wanted to be here, but, circumstances being what they are, we're thankful to be here together, thankful for the circle of comfort, thankful to not be alone.

For Reflection and Discussion

1 Have you seen grief creating distance between you and your peers, coworkers, family, or friends? Do you feel like people understand your pain?

2 Do you feel more connected to people who've experienced loss than you did before you'd experienced loss yourself? If so, think of an example.

3 What's keeping you from reaching out to other people who might have similar experiences? Do you have healthy reasons to hold back or are you making excuses? Make a list of people you know who've suffered loss. Pick one or two names from the list and plan how you'll reach out to them.

4 What does it look like for you to receive comfort in your suffering? How are you at reaching out to others for comfort, compassion, and connection?

5 Are you at a point where you have some comfort to share? What could you say to someone who's lost a loved one that might bring them real comfort?

Resources

Miller, Donald. *A Million Miles in a Thousand Years: How I Learned to Live a Better Story.*

This is not a book about grief, but it is a book about how to live a life. I found, as I tried to rebuild my life after my brother died, that this book was more helpful than almost anything else. Be sure to check out the chapter, "The Pain Will Bind Us."

Griefshare.org

GriefShare is an organization devoted to creating safe places for the grieving to find comfort and connection via weekly group sessions. GriefShare also offers books, videos, and resources to help with your grief journey.

Junger, Sebastian. *Tribe: On Homecoming and Belonging.*

This short book makes the case for suffering as a powerful point of connection, arguing from the angle of a soldier's experience in war. I recommend this book all the time, especially to people on the hunt for belonging.

10

Looking for Light: The Gift of Gratitude

My brother was born premature. My mother, seven months pregnant, woke in the night covered in blood. In the dark she thought she'd wet the bed. In the bathroom, looking at the aborted placenta in the toilet and the smears on the tile floor, she realized something was terribly wrong. She thought she'd lost the baby. My father, just twenty-one, carried her to the car, his prized Camaro. Her blood stained the seats.

Doctors said the baby would probably die during birth, that my mother, nineteen at the time, should consider aborting for her own safety. He and she both survived the trauma of delivery, but Bobby stayed in the NICU for months, always on the verge of not making it. My earliest memory is of visiting him in the hospital. It's fuzzy now, and I can't be sure what I remember isn't a conglomeration of other people's stories, but what I think I remember is getting off the elevator at the hospital with my dad, maybe my grandfather, and seeing a picture of a baby on a poster, a baby covered in wires and tubes, and the adult holding me telling me, "That's your little brother." Years later my mother would tell me he'd been NICU baby of the week. Soon enough Bobby would be Gerber-baby cute—white blond hair, rosy cheeks, blue-gray eyes—but then and for a few months, he looked like a frog.

I don't know what it's like to shuffle back and forth to the hospital to see your baby, to go to sleep at night and know someone else will be answering his cries, to wonder if you'll ever get to bring him home and give him a bath. These days hospitals are more generous with mothers and fathers and the time they can spend with their too-small newborns. Then, thirty-five years ago, there was much enforced separation. I suspect this is why when my mother finally had the chance to hold him she held him so close.

A week after he died, twenty years after he'd lived, lying on the floor beside my mother on her couch, I listened to her recount those early months and memories. I stared at the white lights of the Christmas tree, remembering how tenderly she'd loved him, all the times she'd protected him from me, his too-tough sister. She said, "I'm so thankful I got to have your brother for twenty years. I didn't deserve that gift."

WHO DOES that? Who, less than two weeks after losing her son—a son who'd never see his twenty-first birthday, a son who couldn't legally rent a car or buy a beer—who thanks God for the gift of a measly twenty years? I didn't exactly understand it at the time, her posture of gratitude, her eyes to see light in the dark, but I knew her words seemed holy and good. Since then, I've held onto this moment the way a little girl on a scary road holds her flashlight. My mother's example of gratitude lights the path.

Loss is not a gift.

In some ways, this entire book grows out of my efforts to find things to be thankful for in the middle of my pain. I'm sure you've noticed; I say the word "gift" quite a lot, possibly too much for your taste. Just to be clear, with all this talk of gifts, loss is not a gift. I don't believe for a moment that God blessed you with the death of your dad or wife or child. Death, as we've said already, is a thief, God's enemy, a curse. You know that. Know that I know it, too.

But now that we're here, now that loss is said and done, and grief has become the air we breathe, what now? Can we look for gifts now? I think so. I'm convinced they're here.

Good for You

Early on in the grieving process, even before the funeral rolls around, thanksgiving creeps in among the tears. Husbands say, "She was so kind, ever sacrificing herself for the family." Mothers say, "He was a beautiful child, always making me laugh." Friends say, "She showed up for me when no one else did." Coworkers say, "His smiling face lit up the office." Partly this is a remembering, trying to sketch a portrait of a person while the memory of their face is still fresh. But partly it's an exercise in thanksgiving. Aren't we thankful we have something good to say? Aren't we thankful this person blessed us or helped us or made our lives brighter? In our sadness we're reminded of our past joy. This loss inspires us to remember what was good and recount its goodness.

Loss inspires us to remember what was good and recount its goodness.

In this early season of grief, we direct our feelings of gratitude toward the person who died. We thank them for being a person we can remember fondly. Some people, of course, leave us little to be thankful for, and in that case, thanksgiving is replaced with anger, guilt, or regret. Most of the time, however, feelings of gratitude toward the departed are natural and easy.

Often, particularly in the case of accidental deaths or the death of a young person, we find ourselves thankful we're still living, thankful we're healthy, thankful it wasn't us in the car that hit the tree. We don't usually direct that thanks to any particular origin. Thanking God we're alive might imply that God's to blame for those who're dead.

Gratitude toward God takes time.

It's my experience that feeling gratitude toward God takes time. With God, our feelings are often complicated. We wonder why he didn't intervene to save our loved one, why he allows death at all in a post-resurrection world. We don't understand pain, disease, hatred, accidents—all of these things reigning on earth in direct opposition to all God says he stands for. It can be hard to thank God for anything, our hands so full of disappointment.

But it's precisely because of this disillusionment and disappointment that thanksgiving is valuable in grief. God is hard to see in the fog, but that doesn't mean he's not there. It means, if you want to see him, you'll need to look on purpose.

God is hard to see in the fog, but that doesn't mean he's not there. It means, if you want to see him, you'll need to look on purpose.

In closing his first letter to the Christians living in Thessalonica, the apostle Paul writes, "Rejoice always, pray continually, give thanks in all circumstances; for this is God's will for you in Christ

Jesus" (5:16–18). This is a hard verse for people who're suffering, but it's people who're suffering who need it most. Here Paul offers direction for enduring difficult things: rejoice, pray, give thanks—always, continually, in all circumstances. He says thanksgiving isn't just for people living in the sunshine. Thanksgiving is for people in the shadows, too. He encourages us to say with David, *Yea though I walk through the valley of the shadow of death* . . . thank you.

Rejoice always, pray continually, give thanks in all circumstances; for this is God's will for you in Christ Jesus.

Ann Voskamp writes in her book, *One Thousand Gifts: A Dare to Live Fully Right Where You Are*,

> I have lived pain, and my life can tell: I only deepen the wound of the world when I neglect to give thanks for early light dappled through leaves and the heavy perfume of wild roses in early July and the song of crickets on humid nights and the rivers that run and the stars that rise and the rain that falls and all the good things that a good God gives.[2]

Voskamp opens her book on giving thanks with an account of her sister's tragic childhood death. She's not blind to the darkness. Instead, the darkness she's seen compels her to see and mark the light. This world, full of hard things, is also full of beauty and joy, life, hope, healing, love, and loyalty. Our grief, while devastating, ought not turn the whole world to night. Thanksgiving is an exercise in letting in the light.

Our grief, while devastating, ought not turn the whole world to night. Thanksgiving is an exercise in letting in the light.

In recent years psychologists and social scientists have spent a great deal of energy studying the practice of thanksgiving—the

Resolve to spend most of your time in thanksgiving and praising God. If you cannot do it with the joy that you should, yet do it as you can. You have not the power of your comforts; but have you no power of your tongues? Say not that you are unfit for thanks and praises unless you have a praising heart and were the children of God; for every man, good and bad, is bound to praise God, and to be thankful for all that he hath received, and to do it as well as he can, rather than leave it undone. . . . Doing it as you can is the way to be able to do it better. Thanksgiving stirreth up thankfulness in the heart.[1]

—*The Practical Works of Richard Baxter*

combination of both identifying good things in one's life and attributing those good things to some outside source (another person, a higher power). Leading the way in this field is professor of psychology Robert Emmons. Emmons and his team have studied more than one thousand people, ages eight to eighty, and have found that people who practice gratitude (even those newly trained in gratitude) have stronger immune systems, lower blood pressure, and more energy than those who don't. They're also happier, more compassionate, and more outgoing. Thankful people sleep better, too.[3]

People who practice gratitude (even those newly trained in gratitude) have stronger immune systems, lower blood pressure, and more energy than those who don't. They're also happier, more compassionate, and more outgoing. Thankful people sleep better, too.

Emmons, reflecting on why gratitude achieved such significant results in his study participants, proposed several reasons for its effectiveness. Most interesting as we consider how to embrace and endure our seasons of grief is Emmons's assertion that people who practice gratitude are significantly more stress resistant. He writes, "There's a number of studies showing that in the face of serious trauma, adversity, and suffering, if people have a grateful disposition, they'll recover more quickly. I believe gratitude gives people a perspective from which they can interpret negative life events and help them guard against post-traumatic stress and lasting anxiety."[4]

The practice of thanksgiving—of combing our lives for gifts, of seeing them, naming them, and labeling them as gifts from our Creator and Father—gives us the perspective we need to withstand the pain and empowers us to experience God's generous, peace-giving presence.

Gratitude gives people a perspective from which they can interpret negative life events and help them guard against post-traumatic stress and lasting anxiety.

On hard days, days when I hit the snooze button ten times, days when I watch too much TV and talk to too few people, days when all I want to think about are the things I miss and the things I'll never get to do because he's gone, on those days I force myself to

> The unthankful heart . . . discovers no mercies; but the thankful heart . . . will find, in every hour, some heavenly blessings.
>
> —Henry Ward Beecher, *Leadership*[5]

practice thanksgiving. I'll gather paper and a pen or walk to my kitchen, grab a window marker, and write on my back door. I make myself name one good thing, one gift, one spark of life or joy, the more specific the better. I write, "Thank you, God, for my girls, for two dozen questions on the way home from school, children eager to know." I look around at my home, my backyard. "Thank you, God, for fewer ants, for the friend who helped us make the yard safe for bare feet." I relive my day. "Thank you, God, for warm socks to wear on cold floors." I try not to take things for granted. "Thank you, God, for food in the pantry. Thank you for lungs that work. Thank you for air to breathe."

I make myself name one good thing, one gift, one spark of life or joy.

Most days this practice is like walking through the house throwing open curtains, light breaking through, illuminating and making lovely. But some days I get to feeling like the bad things weigh more, like the gifts are small and the pain is big. On those days I write my pains first. I say all the things that are wrong and bad and sad and not the way I want them to be. And then, having emptied my pockets of rocks, I try thanksgiving again. Inevitably, the blessings list is longer, even when it only includes the expected things like breath and shelter, grace, God's presence, and the promise of eternal life.

Here on this page, speaking to you there in real life and real pain, I don't want to say, "Cheer up! Things are good!" But I do want to say, "Don't let the dark blind you to the light." Thanksgiving isn't a panacea. Nor is it some placebo, a mind trick to get you better. Thanksgiving is the brave and wise recognition of what is true. You are hurting. *And* you are blessed. Very blessed. Live in the dappled light.

Thanksgiving is the brave and wise recognition of what is true. You are hurting. *And* you are blessed. Very blessed. Live in the dappled light.

Get started practicing thanksgiving. Look back at your day. Where can you see the hand of God? Make a list of things you're thankful for. When you've finished, take a minute to assess how you feel.

> We can only be said to be alive in those moments when our hearts are conscious of our treasures.
>
> —Thornton Wilder, *The Woman of Andros*[6]

Eucharist

I'm writing this chapter on Good Friday. It's a perfect day here in Round Rock, Texas—68 degrees, sun shining, trees blooming. It's an ill-fitting day for cross meditation. But here I am staring at an image of the Isenheim Altarpiece and reading Psalm 22.

This altarpiece I'm considering is more than five hundred years old. It depicts the crucifixion of Christ in excruciating detail. It's said the artist painted Jesus this way, so graphically in pain, in order to connect with the many sick and suffering men and women who would view it in the Monastery of St. Anthony, known for the monks' faithful care of plague sufferers, people with nowhere else to go, people in constant pain. It's hard to look at this Jesus, vulnerable, hurting, victim. I know later he will be victorious, but here, here he's defeated. At the bottom of the altar friends hold Jesus's body, wrapping it for burial. I suppose this additional scene, a fast forward to what happens next, exists to remind us Jesus did not escape death.

Jesus did not escape death.

I have the altarpiece pulled up on my phone and my Bible open beside it to Psalm 22, the psalm Jesus famously quotes on the cross: "My God, my God, why hast thou forsaken me?" The psalm is a song for sufferers—first sung by David, then sung by a Jesus who, barely able to gasp, groaned a single stanza. I think he'd have sung the whole thing if he'd had the breath. I'm not alone in that thought. Psalm 22 is considered to be a messianic prophecy, a song that makes some sense coming from David but makes more sense from the lips of Christ. When Jesus spoke that first line, it's like he told the gathered crowd, turn in your songbooks to Psalm 22.

My God, my God, why hast thou forsaken me?

Some call this song a lament, heavy as it is with complaint and anguish. But unlike most laments, this psalm dedicates a full third of its verses (all of the final ten) to praise and thanksgiving. David and Jesus sing,

> For he has not despised or scorned
> the suffering of the afflicted one;
> he has not hidden his face from him
> but has listened to his cry for help. (v. 24)

He has not hidden his face from him but has listened to his cry for help.

Even on the cross, even dying, even blind to God's presence, Jesus is thanking his Father for what's coming, the deliverance to be accomplished.

Jesus hates the cross. He begs to avoid it. He aches and moans from its grotesque height. *And Jesus sees what God will accomplish through it.* Somehow, Jesus manages thanksgiving *for* the cross *on* the cross.

Somehow, Jesus manages thanksgiving *for* the cross *on* the cross.

Every Sunday my church gathers for the communion meal. We eat unleavened bread and drink grape juice and celebrate together the cross of Christ. It's a strange tradition, the eating of flesh and drinking of blood, the celebration of a death. But alas, this is the tradition our founder began just before his death on the cross. It was his last wish that we'd eat the meal together to remember him: "The Lord Jesus, on the night he was betrayed, took bread, and when he had given thanks, he broke it and said, 'This is my body, which is for you; do this in remembrance of me'" (1 Cor 11:24). Paul would say that in this meal Christians "proclaim the Lord's death until he comes" (v. 26).

The Lord Jesus, on the night he was betrayed, took bread, and when he had given thanks, he broke it and said, "This is my body, which is for you; do this in remembrance of me."

Maybe you don't call this meal communion or the Lord's Supper. Maybe you call it the Eucharist—literally, *the thanksgiving.* You, as a part of the community of Christ, have experience giving thanks for a death—not because the death was good (all death is bad), but because in and through the death, God worked. I don't thank God for Jesus's pain. I don't thank him for the brutality of the soldiers or the ridicule of the crowds or the vinegar on his thirsty lips. But I do thank him for redeeming the pain, for making something beautiful

You, as a part of the community of Christ, have experience giving thanks for a death—not because the death was good (all death is bad), but because in and through the death, God worked.

Gratitude finds its source in all kinds of places, some lovely and some not.

from something essentially and truly hideous. I thank him for refusing to let one drop of blood be wasted.

What's the lesson for me, a sufferer, suspended in grief? I return to Psalm 22 and remember that gratitude finds its source in all kinds of places, some lovely and some not. I remember that though the pain I'm experiencing is terrible, I'm not alone. I remember to call out for God, *"Why have you forsaken me?"* To call out knowing he hears me, my call itself a form of hopeful thanks. Jesus, even in his undelivered state, gives thanks for a God who "has not hidden his face" (Ps 22:24).

More

I asked my friend Georgine how thanksgiving had transformed her grief, and she told me a story about her brother dying and how hard she'd taken it, how she'd paced the halls of her house wailing in angry prayer. She said, "One day, while pacing, I glanced at a baby picture of Mitch on the wall." Mitch is her son, my friend, as good a human as I know. Georgine told me she'd named Mitch, "Mitchell James" after her brother Jim back when her brother first faced serious health struggles, colon cancer and liver disease. They weren't sure he would live then, and Georgine had wanted him to know he had a namesake. But that was twenty years ago. Baby Mitch was now a grown man attending a funeral, Jim's funeral, in a suit and tie.

She realized looking at Mitch's picture on the wall, that when her brother had first gotten sick she'd prayed like Hezekiah did, that he would get fifteen more years. She'd prayed specifically for those fifteen years. She said to me,

> Reflecting on the fact that we indeed got those fifteen plus years of having Jim around, I couldn't help but go from mourning to joy, expressing abundant thanksgiving for what now seemed like bonus years with Jim. From then on, my perspective changed. Still sad, still missing Jim, but always thankful for the years we had him.

God, help me let go of my expectations and accept the gifts that you give me each day, knowing that there is beauty and wonder in each act of life.

—Melody Beattie, Gratitude: *Inspirations*[7]

I heard her story and thought of my mother, thankful for a son she almost lost but got to keep for twenty years.

I'm thinking of what it would look like to give thanks in my grief…

I think of my miscarriages and thank God they were early, that I didn't have to go the hospital, that only a few people knew, and they were the best people to know, loving and kind. I thank God for a perfect name for our first child and first child lost—Canaan, promised land. I thank God for health insurance and for a husband who is tender and optimistic.

I think of losing my grandfathers, both in one month, men who helped raise me, men I adored. I thank God I had the chance to sit with one the night before he died, reading from Romans, listening to his last words, "The Lord is my shepherd." I thank God the other didn't have to suffer before he died, that the death was quick and painless though unexpected. I thank God I had the chance to deliver the eulogy at one funeral and didn't have to deliver it at the other. I thank God for family to grieve alongside. I thank God for good memories in skyscraper-sized stacks.

I think of losing my grandmother when I was little, watching her dying on our couch. I'm thankful to God for the chance to watch a woman suffer with grace. And I'm thankful to have weathered something so hard so young.

The last time I saw my brother in the flesh, living and breathing and cracking sarcastic jokes, we ate pancakes and made small-talk at a Cracker Barrel. He was headed home to Florida for Thanksgiving.

Consider the circumstances of your grief.

- Where is God making good from evil?
- What comforts has he afforded you in your pain?
- What are you learning?
- Who has he sent to love and serve you?
- Try to identify the light in your darkness. Thank God for it.

It would be my last Thanksgiving with a sibling. But it wouldn't be the last time I'd give thanks for one.

I thank God for that kid almost every day. I'm thankful to God for twenty years with my best friend. I'm thankful to have grown up with someone who pushed me and challenged me and encouraged me and comforted me. I'm thankful to God for a rival and a partner. I'm thankful that even right now, fifteen years after he died, I can roll footage in my mind of him laughing, his grin lopsided, his eyes closed, his hair caked in too much gel.

I'm also thankful for the circumstances of his death—that he was sober (and that no one ever wondered if he was), that no one else was injured in the accident. Though he died on a sixteen-hour road trip, he was almost home when he hit the tree, and we didn't have to travel far to collect his body and things. I'm thankful too that he and I hadn't fought recently, that he wasn't married and didn't have kids.

Beyond all of that, I'm thankful for what God's accomplished through my brother's death, what God's made possible through this exhausting, torturous season of grief. I'm wiser, more resilient, able to help others. I'm less tethered to success or wealth or any of the other passing pleasures of this place. I'm not afraid to die. I think about heaven a lot; I often have eyes to see the unseen. I'm close to God, and I look more like him than I ever did before Bobby died.

I'm not glad Bobby died. Never. I'd undo it without a second thought. But as I recall Paul's words to give thanks in all

> To be grateful is to recognize the Love of God in everything He has given us—and He has given us everything. Every breath we draw is a gift of His love, every moment of existence is a grace, for it brings with it immense graces from Him.
>
> Gratitude therefore takes nothing for granted, is never unresponsive, is constantly awakening to new wonder and to praise of the goodness of God. For the grateful person knows that God is good, not by hearsay but by experience. And that is what makes all the difference.
>
> —Thomas Merton, *Thoughts in Solitude*[8]

circumstances and as I think of Christ on the cross and the Eucharist meal we eat each week, I'm comfortable giving thanks—not for his death exactly, but rather for all God's done (and will do) in and through it.

For Reflection and Discussion

1 Think of five things you're thankful for about the person you've lost. List them here.

2 How does Paul's invitation to "give thanks in all circumstances" make you feel? Does thanksgiving come easy to you?

3 In what ways has grief caused you to be disappointed or disillusioned with God?

4 How do the cross and the practice of giving thanks in the Eucharist meal inform your suffering? What would it look like for you to follow Christ's example and give thanks in your suffering?

Resources

Voskamp, Ann. *One Thousand Gifts: A Dare to Live Fully Right Where You Are.*

Hands down, this is my favorite book on gratitude. Voskamp recognizes that thanksgiving isn't a simple, delightful practice for happy people, but rather it's a hard, essential discipline for the suffering. Much of what I know about thanksgiving I learned from this book.

Robinson, Josie. *The Gratitude Jar: A Simple Guide to Creating Miracles.*

While Voskamp's book is rooted in Scripture and a mature faith, this one comes from a less rooted and complicated place. A quicker read (perhaps oversimplified), but still largely true and helpful, this is a book for encouragement and inspiration. It's the kind of book you pass on to friends.

Emmons, Robert. *Gratitude Works! A 21-Day Program for Creating Emotional Prosperity.*

Emmons has written numerous books on the topic of gratitude. I like this one because it includes a practical plan for incorporating gratitude into your life. If either you still need to be convinced of the power of gratitude or if you need help making it a habit, this is a great resource.

11

Rebuilding: The Gift of a New Normal

Recently a friend of mine lost her younger sister suddenly and unexpectedly. Her sister had gone into the hospital for some seemingly simple problem. The doctors kept her overnight, said they'd treat her and release her in the morning. And then, for reasons still undetermined, she died. She left behind two little kids, a husband, and her thirty-four-year-old sister and best friend.

She messaged me the other day, this grieving sister, and told me about having dinner with her parents, how strange it was without her sister there, how no one knew quite what to say, how everyone always ended up in tears. She asked, "Will we ever feel like a family again?" I sighed from behind the computer screen.

Less than a month after my brother died, my parents and I took a trip to New York City. They had time off work and a little extra insurance money. My mom had always wanted to go. And we all needed a distraction.

We shared a tiny hotel room in Times Square. The first night we were there, it snowed. I'd only seen snow two or three times in my life. I saw it through the hotel window and said, "Let's go look at it!" My mom was too sad to go downstairs. My dad went with me, and we stood silently side-by-side on the sidewalk letting flakes fall on our swollen, tear-tired faces.

I don't remember a lot from that trip. I remember how we sat at meals without anything to say, how we wandered from site to site, checking things off a list, how we went to bed early every night. I remember getting in a whisper fight in an art gallery. The whole trip was off, wrong, incomplete without Bobby.

So when my friend said "Will we ever feel like family again?" Will it ever be the way it used to be? I knew exactly what she meant.

Will it ever be the way it used to be?

THEY SAY in counseling that after a great loss a person has to learn to accept a "new normal," the idea being that the "old normal" can't be recovered. It's gone. We understand this, but that doesn't mean we like it (or accept it). Recently I asked a few hundred people what they most wanted in their grief. The number one answer? For things to be normal again.

After a great loss a person has to learn to accept a "new normal."

The idea of a new normal means that grievers have to stop waiting for the reappearance of what used to be and instead start walking forward. A new normal requires new choices and new habits, new hobbies, new friends, new routines. This new normal is pushy, demanding, uncomfortable, and occasionally heartbreaking. It seems like a betrayal of some kind to keep living without your brother or dad or daughter, to make plans and take trips and make decisions. Sometimes it feels like a betrayal to watch the next episode of her favorite show.

Remembering my own old normal—pickup basketball and singing in the car, family wrestling tournaments, road trip games, and uproarious laughter—I said to my grieving friend, "It will always be different from what it was, and that will always be sad."

It will always be different from what it was, and that will always be sad.

"Eventually though," I told her, "it will be happy *and* sad."

"Eventually though," I told her, "it will be happy *and* sad."

Mixed Feelings

In Psalm 137 the people of Israel mourn the fallen city of Jerusalem. Now slaves in faraway Babylon, they lament the loss of their home, identity, and way of life. They cry:

> By the rivers of Babylon we sat and wept
> when we remembered Zion.
> There on the poplars
> we hung our harps,
> for there our captors asked us for songs,
> our tormentors demanded songs of joy;
> they said, "Sing us one of the songs of Zion!"
> How can we sing the songs of the Lord
> while in a foreign land?

This picture of God's people grieving their homeland, hanging their harps in the trees, abandoning joy, refusing to sing, is heartbreaking. And also familiar—like the way I felt driving to the airport the day Bobby died, wanting to roll down my window and yell at the passing cars, "What are you doing? Stop laughing. Stop working. Stop everything. Don't you know my brother's died?" In this moment, the people of Israel must feel like everything is over, like nothing will ever be good again.

I bet they felt as if singing was betraying what they'd lost. I bet they hated their "new normal."

Decades later we find God's people, some of them, returning to Jerusalem to rebuild the city of God after the exile. They start with the temple. On the day the foundation of the temple of the Lord was laid, the priests and Levites gathered to sing praise to the Lord. They sang,

> He is good;
> his love toward Israel endures forever.

We need not be afraid of the real world. We can live in it again. We can even love it again.

—Granger E. Westberg, *Good Grief*[1]

Ezra recorded the people's reaction: "And all the people gave a great shout of praise to the Lord, because the foundation of the house of the Lord was laid" (Ezra 3:11).

How long had it been since a shout of praise echoed through the streets of Jerusalem? Imagine the Israelites all gathered—old men and young women, children clinging to hands and legs trying not to get lost in the crowds—all of them here to witness the beginning of a new Israel. This moment seems perfect for pulling the harps from the trees.

But not everyone sees the moment that way. Instead, "many of the older priests and Levites and family heads, who had seen the former temple, wept aloud when they saw the foundation of this temple being laid" (v. 12). It seems the older men, when they see the foundation, can't bear it. Perhaps it's too small or too plain, nothing like Solomon's temple, so grand and elaborate. Perhaps seeing this slab of rock brings back memories. Perhaps it reminds them of the city's fall, of the family they lost, the children murdered in the streets, the burning city of God. Perhaps this new foundation reminds those who lost everything of everything they lost.

Ezra describes the scene, the old men weeping and the young men praising, this way: "No one could distinguish the sound of the shouts of joy from the sound of weeping, because the people made so much noise. And the sound was heard far away" (v. 13).

Building something new in place of something old isn't easy. The new normal doesn't look right or feel right. It itches, provokes, unsettles. At first, facing it makes the grieving harder. But if we'll push through, endure and embrace the change, and keep building, we'll find ourselves standing on a firm foundation, crying and praising, both.

Building something new in place of something old isn't easy.

This year my parents, my husband, my two girls and I traveled to Santa Fe, New Mexico. We packed ourselves into a car, drove ten hours, and arrived at the city square just in time for dancing. On the trip, we swam in a hot spring beside the Rio Grande. We laughed over ice cream, explored an opera house, toured an alien museum, and hiked to the top of a mountain. My dad played cards with my daughters at the dinner table. My mom brushed their hair.

My friend asked me, "Will we ever feel like family again?"

Yes, you will. You will if you keep living—if, as a part of grieving the life you lost together, you painstakingly build a new one. If you're willing to push through the tears and pain and awkwardness and not-quite-right-ness and disappointment, you can turn this new normal into something good, something you'd be sad to lose.

I told my friend, the one who wanted normal back, "Your family has to make new memories. You need new traditions and trips to places your sister never went. You need pictures without your sister in them." I said, "In the coming years you'll love each other in new ways. You'll help each other and teach each other and laugh together, and slowly, purposefully, you'll build a new set of inside jokes, family jargon, and happy memories. Over the years those memories will stack up until eventually there are more new, happy memories than sad ones."

That's how it worked for my family. Year after year we stacked things: new friendships, fulfilling work, vacations, children and grandchildren, moments of worship. . . . One day the stack was so big the scales tipped and the new normal really did seem normal. And happy.

This past year I woke up on December 13 and launched into my daily routine. I checked on my kids, already up and eating Cheerios from the box. I made coffee. I reviewed the planner. I texted my daughter's piano teacher. I wrote an email. I read my Bible. At some point I checked Facebook on my phone and found a few messages from friends who'd remembered it was December 13 and offered words of comfort.

I had forgotten it was December 13, the day my brother died.

For me, this was the moment I realized life had finally become "normal." For the first time in thirteen years, hearing that date, December 13, didn't crush me. I actually felt fine. I put down the phone and helped my daughter with her math.

If you're willing to push through the tears and pain and awkwardness and not-quite-right-ness and disappointment, you can turn this new normal into something good, something you'd be sad to lose.

Over the years those memories will stack up until eventually there are more new, happy memories than sad ones.

Looking back, I can see I've been building something. God and I, my family, my friends, we all built a mountain of new experiences. And we're building them still. Those experiences bring healing. This present, so full of people and plans, brings wholeness, purpose, peace, joy, life.

Instructions for Building

A few years ago, I sat in a living room in a chair three feet from a friend who'd recently lost his wife to cancer. I say recently, but it'd been almost a year. What's a year when you've lived a whole life together?

The house was full of her—pictures on the wall, her art on the table, hardly anything altered since her death. I imagined her sitting beside us—or up, certainly up, offering us food, scurrying around to find some book her husband John wanted to show me. I imagined she hadn't died but was napping in the back bedroom or outside tending to the goats. Everything seemed just as it had before.

But then he showed me a YouTube video on his new Apple computer. John was on YouTube (and Facebook, too). I smiled wide as he clicked open the video window. Five years ago John didn't own a computer. He wrote his sermon notes on old church directory pages. Earlier he'd shown me pictures he'd taken on his new Nikon DSLR, something he'd always put off buying despite his love for and remarkable talent in photography. He didn't know how to use it yet, not like he wanted to. But he was learning.
The pictures were of Petra, in southern Jordan. And Israel. A few months after his wife died, John hopped a plane to the holy lands with friends, a place he'd devoted years and thousands of hours to studying. I looked at pictures of camels. He told me about crawling to the spot where Jesus was born.

And then he said he'd be in the Marshall Islands this summer. The Grand Canyon in the spring.

"The best thing for being sad," replied Merlin, beginning to puff and blow, "is to learn something. That's the only thing that never fails."

—T. H. White, *The Once and Future King*[2]

All of this—the spontaneous traveling, the social media, the luxury and excitement of a still-to-be-figured-out camera—all of it was new. And who would have guessed it of a sixty-year-old man wading through grief?

I realized that while so much was the same, a lot had changed.

He said to me, "Every so often everything crumbles, and we have to build something new."

What does it look like to build something new? Does it mean knocking everything down? Does it mean throwing out every good thing from the past? Not at all. My friend John, for example, kept much of his life just as it always had been. He stayed in the home he and his wife had built with their own hands. He kept the house the same way she'd decorated it. He liked it. He did his hair the same way he always had and ate mostly the same food.

Every so often everything crumbles, and we have to build something new.

But some things changed, and some of those changes were hard. John had to learn to cook. He had to figure out how to do all the things his wife had done at the church he pastored, jobs he didn't even realize she'd done until he showed up on a Sunday and no one was there to do them. He had to figure out how to grandparent alone. He had to shop for clothes and eat dinner in a booth alone at his favorite restaurant.

Some of the changes weren't so bad, though. John had more money now and more time. He was more flexible now that he didn't have to work around his wife's schedule. He could stay up late figuring out his camera and sleep in if he wanted. He realized when his wife died that almost every facet of his life had been tailored to fit his partnership with her. Now that he didn't have a partner, his life could be tailored to fit him.

This new life he built was beautiful. He'd rather have had his old life. But if he had to have a new one, he might as well build one he liked.

It's always shocking to watch everything crumble, and it's always hard to build something new. But the gift of rebuilding is the chance to choose. What you build from the wreckage of loss is up to you. If grief requires change, embrace the change and make it good in whatever ways you might.

The gift of rebuilding is the chance to choose. What you build from the wreckage of loss is up to you. If grief requires change, embrace the change and make it good in whatever ways you might.

As you imagine a new normal, as you seek new experiences and new friendships, as you build a post-loss life, ask yourself questions like these:

What do I have time for now that I didn't have time for before?

What freedom do I have that I didn't have before?

What do I enjoy doing that I didn't do as much as I would like before?

What kinds of people do I enjoy being around? Are there people I avoided before because of my loved one's preferences? How might I reconnect with those people?

What parts of my old life do I want to be sure to carry on even without my loved one?

The closer you are to a person, the more your normal life shifts upon their death. For me, losing an adult brother didn't radically change my everyday, but it did have a huge impact on the way I planned my future. Before my brother died I imagined life on a cul-de-sac two houses down from his. I imagined big family birthday parties in backyards and unbreakable Christmas traditions. After Bobby died, that life unavailable, my husband and I moved across the country to Brooklyn to start a church. We didn't know a soul. We'd likely never have even considered the move with Bobby alive. But when Bobby died, we had to build something new. What we built was a gift.

I think of the handful of new "brothers" I've made over the years, young men I had the space and attention to love: an ex-student who turned into a lifelong friend, preaching interns we have to

> The melody that the loved one played upon the piano of your life will never be played quite that way again, but we must not close the keyboard and allow the instrument to gather dust. We must seek out other artists of the spirit, new friends who gradually will help us to find the road to life again, who will walk the road to life again, who will walk that road with us.
>
> —Rabbi Joshua Liebman, *Peace of Mind*[3]

push out the door at midnight, so we can get some sleep (though we wish they'd just stay and drink more of our coffee and tell us about the books they're reading), a cousin who woke up at 5 a.m. to buy the very first copy of my first book. . . . My kids call almost a dozen people uncle. I thank God for that. For a new normal full of new brothers.

Obviously I still miss my first brother. But not in an always-painful way. Not in a way that makes me want to go back. Not in a way that keeps me trapped in a past I'll never move beyond. Not in a way that gets in the way of living an abundant life.

Grief doesn't have to last forever. Of course, you will always miss the person you love. But the missing will fade into the background while your life—your beautiful, exciting, Jesus-shaped life—expands.

If you choose to let grief go unchecked, if you decide to stop living because someone you loved isn't living, then grief will persist. It won't stop. It won't get better. It will only get worse. It will crush you under its oppressive weight.

Don't let it do that.

Have hope. Believe that what's to come can be better than what was. And do something, build something new.

Have hope. Believe that what's to come can be better than what was. And do something, build something new.

Start a tradition like my friend Bob did after his brother died and left two little kids behind. He baked cookies with his niece and nephew, smiling through tears, not because he wanted to bake cookies, but because he knew baking cookies through tears *now* was a step toward baking cookies with joy *later*.

Lean into friendships you've ignored or let lapse. Plan a friends trip like Diane did after her brother died. She organized a weekend at the beach with her best friends, not running away from her pain but countering it with something that didn't hurt so much.

Do what the apostles did after Jesus died and rose and ascended, and get moving. Without Jesus, their new normal looked like launching a movement of love and light, doing the work Jesus would have been so proud to see them doing.

What the apostles experienced on the day Jesus went up to heaven wasn't so unlike what I experienced when my brother died. Like the apostles on their hill, I stood on a beach with my friends staring into the ocean, wondering what comes next, asking myself, "Will I ever be happy and whole again?"

Why do you stand here looking into the sky?

An angel stepped in to stop the apostles from *their* nervous staring. He asked, "Why do you stand here looking into the sky?" The apostles answered by going to Jerusalem and starting something new.

Why do *you* stand here looking for what's gone?

What new thing might you go and do?

Why do *you* stand here looking for what's gone?

What new thing might you go and do?

Everything New

The last book of the Bible should be a conclusion, but instead it's a beginning. Throughout the book of Revelation we find God doing brand-new things. His people sing new songs and get new names. God creates a new Jerusalem, and not just a new city, a whole new heaven and new earth. And then, right at the close of John's vision of what is both the end and beginning of time, Jesus speaks from the throne. I read his words, and I'm sure they're just for me. Maybe you think they're just for you. Surely, they're the words we the grieving most need to hear. He says, talking about God and what God will certainly do in the not-too-far-away, "He will wipe every tear from their eyes. There will be no more death or mourning or crying or pain, for the old order of things has passed away."

He will wipe every tear from their eyes. There will be no more death or mourning or crying or pain, for the old order of things has passed away.

No more death.

No more mourning.

No more crying. Or pain.

Death, mourning, crying, pain—that was your old normal.

Jesus says, "I am making everything new!"

For Reflection and Discussion

1 List the things you miss from your "old normal." What parts of your old life will you never get back?

2 What does your "new normal" look like so far? What hard things will you need to get used to? Which can you move past?

3 Are you resistant to the idea of change? If so, why? What's your plan for navigating the inevitable changes that come with loss?

4 What do you want your new life to look like? Who do you want to be? How do you want to spend your time?

5 How did the picture of my friend John's life after his wife's death make you feel? Did you relate? Were you envious? Did you feel like he'd moved on too soon? Root around in your heart for a second. What do you think your reaction says about where you are in grief?

Resources

Westberg, Granger E. *Good Grief.*

This short, helpful book is devoted to the idea that grief can be good, achieving in us a transformation. Westberg says, "Grief can be counted among the great deepening experiences of life."

Miller, Donald. *A Million Miles in a Thousand Years: How I Learned to Live a Better Story.*

This is not a book about grief, but it is a book about how to live a life. I found, as I tried to rebuild my life after my brother died, that this book was more helpful than almost anything else.

Hislop, Victoria, ed. *Loss*.

This compilation of stories about grief is entirely composed by female writers. Each one prods, pokes, or comforts. The two I find most instructive in loss are "The Merry Widow" by Margaret Drabble and "Father, Father" by Susan Hill. Each story represents an entirely different way of handling grief, but both deal with disorientation and rebuilding.

12

Cultivating Joy: The Gift of Celebration

For some, grief is like a pin poking a hole in their bag of joy; they hold their hands under the hole trying to catch it as it drains, with no luck. Others don't try. They feel paralyzed watching it bleed out.

I know people who used to be the life of the party, but now they're not. Now, after their wife's death or their child's death or their best friend's death, they're serious and quiet and usually sad.

A friend tells me his wife is a totally different person now that their child's gone. Everything reminds her of him. Every previous source of joy is turned to sadness. Another friend says her dad feels like there's nothing to live for with his wife gone. He says this to his daughter, who holds his granddaughter, and it stings to hear, but it's how he feels. Another friend doesn't know who to be funny with anymore. Her partner in pranks and silly videos and terrible impressions is gone.

To make it all worse, not only has the joy gone, the memories of a time full of joy linger, taunting us from the other side of the grave. It's said the Greek playwright Aeschylus wrote, "There is no pain so great as the memory of joy in present grief." That seems like something a writer of tragedies would say.

Many mourners assume despair is the inevitability of grief, that after a loss joy will lessen or dull or disappear in the face of pain. We imagine joy and grief as poles, and ourselves in constant flux between them. After a loved one dies, we find ourselves pulled toward grief, and consequently away from joy. If we have joy we don't have grief. If we have grief we don't have joy.

That assessment, that grief robs us of joy, is certainly common, but it's not always true. As we'll see, not only can joy and grief coexist, grief can become the door through which we fully access the joy only God can offer.

I'D BEEN married for fifteen months when Bobby died. I met my husband, Justin, at a church event when I was thirteen and he was fifteen. I liked his smile. He liked the way my hair smelled. We fell fast in love and never turned back. He is my perfect opposite—spontaneous, fun, charming, and entirely even-keeled. He tells stories and jokes with reckless abandon; wherever he goes, laughter trails behind like brushfire.

As we'll see, not only can joy and grief coexist, grief can become the door through which we fully access the joy only God can offer.

Justin basically grew up in my house. Which meant he and Bobby spent a lot of time together. On Wednesday nights Justin would drive over from college to see me (his still-in-high-school girlfriend), spend the night, and drive back in the morning. He and Bobby would cram their lanky, six-foot-tall bodies into the same full-size bed, staying up too late talking and dreaming and laughing (or arguing and trying to push each other off the mattress). In the summers Bobby and Justin worked as deckhands on a pirate ship for tourists out of Clearwater Beach. They dressed up like pirates, battled kids with water guns, told treasure stories, and cleaned toilets. Justin gave Bobby his pirate name, Barnacle Bert. On my wedding day, it was Bobby who stood over Justin's shoulder, smiling his crooked smile, as best man.

On the day my brother died, my husband lost a best friend. Over the years I've often weighed our griefs and determined mine to be most important, heaviest. However, in the last five years or so,

> Among the tales of sorrow and of ruin that came down to us from the darkness of those days there are yet some in which amid weeping there is joy and under the shadow of death light that endures.
>
> —J. R. R. Tolkien, *The Silmarillion*[1v]

I've come to realize how much Justin lost and how generously he carried his grief. The other night, sitting at the dining room table, beginning this chapter on grief and joy, I asked him, "What would you say to people who feel like they lose their joy when someone they love dies? What is it you did to make sure you kept it?" I asked him this because joy is a gift of his. He's helium.

He raised his eyebrows, folds filling his brow, and said, "Honestly, I don't think I actually did anything right." He told me he'd mostly tried to distract himself with temporary pleasures, things that seemed like joy for a minute but weren't really. He said,

> Instead of leaning into healthy practices to fuel joy, I leaned into unhealthy practices. I thought, "I'm happy when things are going well. Things aren't going well now. I can't bring Bobby back to make them better. So I'll make two sandwiches instead of one, and my circumstances will be good for a minute."

We both laughed, because what he'd said was ridiculous. And way too true.

But it made me wonder. I'd always thought of Justin as this joy-soaked guy, always laughing, always up for an adventure, always delightful. "Babe," I asked, "do you think you understood joy before Bobby died?"

He looked at me askance, one eyebrow lifted, mouth closed tight and straight. He thought for a minute.

"Nah."

> Let's allow God to use our tears. Let's plant them and watch them grow.
>
> —Shelley Ramsey, *Grief: A Mama's Unwanted Journey*[2]

He said, "When Bobby died it wasn't that my joy got stolen. It was more like, 'Oops, I hadn't been cultivating joy.'" He said he looked joyful because life had been good and easy. Bobby dying didn't rob him of joy. It just revealed he didn't know where to find it. Not yet.

My Strength

This weekend I spoke to a group of women about joy and grief and told them a story from Nehemiah chapter 8. It's a favorite of mine, one I turn to often, particularly when I'm feeling joyless.

The book of Nehemiah comes just after the book of Ezra, and the story we looked at in the last chapter. Both books grow out of the exile and the return of Israel from Babylon. Ezra tells the story of a small, first wave of returning Israelites. Nehemiah tells the second wave's story. In Ezra the people rebuild the temple. In Nehemiah, they repair the walls of the capital city, Jerusalem. Like Ezra, the book of Nehemiah, named after the man who leads the wall-building project, is a book marked by mixed emotions. It's a complicated thing to come home and find your home in ruins.

Thanks to Nehemiah's faithful leadership and the people's commitment to hard, persistent work, the wall goes up. To celebrate their achievement, Israel gathers for a ceremonial reading of the law by the priest, Ezra:

> Ezra opened the book. All the people could see him because he was standing above them; and as he opened it, the people all stood up. Ezra praised the Lord, the great God; and all the people lifted their hands and responded, "Amen! Amen!" Then they bowed down and worshiped the Lord with their faces to the ground. (8:2, 5–6)

This gathering is remarkable for a host of reasons, not least being the fact that most of the people standing in this city square have never heard the law read before. Growing up in Babylon they likely heard stories of their homeland, their father telling them what grapes taste like back home, their mother describing the olive trees she swung from in the spring. They probably heard stories about God, too, stories about the time God delivered Israel from Egypt, stories about God's messengers and rescuers—Abraham, Moses, King David, Elijah the prophet. But they've never heard these stories straight from the scroll. And they've certainly never heard the

We shake with joy, we shake with grief.

—Mary Oliver, "We Shake with Joy"[3]

Do not grieve, for the joy of the Lord is your strength.

Levitical laws laid out in such exacting precision. Their excitement when Ezra opens the book bubbles up into spontaneous worship.

As Ezra reads, the people's emotions become more complex. Confronted with the fullness of God's love, the weight of God's expectations, and Israel's history of refusing to receive that love or meet those expectations, they're overwhelmed to the point of despair. Nehemiah, Ezra the priest, and the Levites have to stop reading and explaining the text in order to comfort the people, "for all the people had been weeping as they listened to the words of the Law" (8:9).

This isn't a story about grief, not precisely, but it is a story about sadness. The reason we're here, the thing I want you see in your sadness and grief, is what comes next. As the people cry and the Levites wander through the crowd consoling them, Nehemiah clears his throat and says for all to hear, "Go and enjoy choice food and sweet drinks. . . . This day is holy to our Lord. Do not grieve, for the joy of the Lord is your strength" (v. 10). You heard that right. Nehemiah looks at people who're sinking in sadness and tells them, Stop crying. Go throw a party. Eat something delicious. Make a toast.

Are you surprised? I sure was the first (and second) time I read it. Maybe you, like me, find Nehemiah's prescription simplistic and dismissive. This sadness the Israelites feel is justified and deep. Later in the book they'll be called to repent and make restitution for their sin in difficult and sacrificial ways. What they've done wrong is real, and their guilt ought to be heavy. Also, what they've missed in all these years away from God, away from their land, away from their customs and traditions and law, is worthy of their sadness. How dare Nehemiah say, You need a drink!

Maybe we're missing something.

Perhaps Nehemiah isn't dismissing their grief but rather offering them a tool for bearing up under it. When he says "the joy of the Lord is your strength," it's like Nehemiah reminds them of their superpower, this "joy" that enables endurance of (perhaps even victory over) sadness. Nehemiah says, *Don't give in to grief. Fight back with the joy of the Lord.* And what does that joy look like? According to Nehemiah it looks like dinner with friends and family, celebrating the work and presence of God.

I've often thought of joy like champagne bubbles—light, frivolous, a luxury—but Nehemiah reorients my perspective, offering up joy as an ox—robust, serious, a beast of burden. I think of celebrations as frosting on the bread of daily life, empty calories, but Nehemiah offers them up as broccoli and kale, filling us and making us strong.

Joy isn't something grief steals. Joy is a renewable resource, available even in grief, available to help us bear up under it. Celebration isn't something ill-fitting for the mourner. The drinks and the meal, the gathering with friends and family, all of it is commanded here to enable joy, to fill an empty tank.

Joy isn't something grief steals. Joy is a renewable resource, available even in grief, available to help us bear up under it.

Sometimes it takes grief bullying its way into our lives for us to learn how to lean upon joy for strength. Sometimes we have to run out of joy to finally, purposefully seek it.

Sometimes we have to run out of joy to finally, purposefully seek it.

The Source

What brings you joy?

Sunshine. A delicious sandwich. A video of a tiger cuddling an orangutan. Coffee with friends. A good book. A hike. A person. Joy happens when two things align: when our circumstances are good and when we notice and enjoy our circumstances. Joy disappears when either the good things go away or we stop noticing them.

Grief, by definition, is similarly circumstantial. What brings you grief? The loss of joy-bringing circumstances. Or people.

Growing up in church I often heard joy defined as something outside of circumstance, something unshifting in shifting winds. My preacher quoted James, "Consider it pure joy, my brothers and sisters, whenever you face trials of many kinds" (1:2), and said joy

> In my own worst seasons I've come back from the colorless world of despair by forcing myself to look hard, for a long time, at a single glorious thing: a flame of red geranium outside my bedroom window. And then another: my daughter in a yellow dress. And another: the perfect outline of a full, dark sphere behind the crescent moon. Until I learned to be in love with my life again. Like a stroke victim retraining new parts of the brain to grasp lost skills, I have taught myself joy, over and over again.
>
> —Barbara Kingsolver, *High Tide in Tucson*[4]

outlasts hardship. I wonder though if it isn't better to interpret this passage this way: not that joy outlasts the circumstance of hardship but that hardship might be a circumstance that brings joy. *More on that later . . .*

Though we often talk about joy as something we either have or don't have, throughout the Bible joy is connected to experience. Joy blooms when people have reason to rejoice. Consider this quick overview of joy in both the Old and New Testaments:

- Leviticus 9:24, "And when all the people saw it, they shouted for joy." *Here the Israelites find joy when they encounter God's presence.*
- Deuteronomy 16:15, "The Lord your God will bless you in all your harvest and in all the work of your hands, and your joy will be complete." *Here the Israelites find joy in God's blessing.*
- 1 Kings 8:66, "They blessed the king and then went home, joyful and glad in heart for all the good things the Lord had done for his servant David and his people Israel." *Again, joy in blessing.*
- 2 Chronicles 20:27, They "returned joyfully to Jerusalem, for the Lord had given them cause to rejoice over their enemies." *Victory in battle leads to joy.*
- Esther 9:22, ". . . the time when the Jews got relief from their enemies . . . when their sorrow was turned into joy and their mourning into a day of celebration." *Joy in not being killed by their enemies.*
- Psalm 19:8, "The precepts of the Lord are right, giving joy to the heart." *Here Davis finds joy in the law.*

- Psalm 67:4, "May the nations be glad and sing for joy, for you rule the peoples with equity and guide the nations of the earth." *Joy in God's leadership.*
- Psalm 90:14, "Satisfy us in the morning with your unfailing love, that we may sing for joy and be glad all our days." *Joy in experiencing the love of God.*
- Proverbs 15:20, "A wise son brings joy to his father." *Here, joy comes from the gift of a son who's not foolish.*
- Isaiah 12:3, "With joy you will draw water from the wells of salvation." *Joy in salvation.*
- Isaiah 49:13, "Shout for joy, you heavens; rejoice, you earth; burst into song, you mountains! For the Lord comforts his people and will have compassion on his afflicted ones." *Joy in the experience of comfort and compassion.*
- Matthew 28:8, "So the women hurried away from the tomb, afraid yet filled with joy." *Here the women find joy in the hope of Christ's resurrection.*
- John 16:21, "A woman giving birth to a child has pain because her time has come; but when her baby is born she forgets the anguish because of her joy that a child is born into the world." *Joy in the condition of motherhood.*
- Romans 12:12, "Be joyful in hope." *Again, we find joy emanating from a source, in this case, the condition of having hope.*

The point is clear, joy is conditional. You have to have good circumstances to experience joy. Fortunately, as is also abundantly clear in Scripture, with God and in Christ, you always do.

To practice joy is to look for and celebrate God's presence and work. A person who experiences joy is a person on the hunt for what's good, a person who recognizes that, even in despair, she will find God working.

Paul writes to the Philippian Christians, "Rejoice in the Lord always. I will say it again: Rejoice!" (4:4). He says a verse later, Don't be anxious about circumstances or situations. He encourages the Philippians to pray, give thanks, and finally, to engage in this practice of seeing and seeking what's good. He writes, "Whatever is true, whatever is noble, whatever is right, whatever is pure, whatever is lovely, whatever is admirable—if anything is excellent or praiseworthy—think about such things" (v. 8). It's possible for the Christian to rejoice always because there is always something true or excellent to see. This means something to the griever. It means joy isn't something we either have or don't have, a possession to be stolen or returned. Joy is something I can seek and find again and again and again.

> It's possible for the Christian to rejoice always because there is always something true or excellent to see.

When Nehemiah encourages the Israelites to drink sweet drinks and gather with friends, he's encouraging them to look for what's good, to delight in the gift of community, to appreciate their accomplishment in building the wall, and to celebrate the God who brought them back and welcomes them home. Are things still bad? Yes. Do those circumstances merit grief? Yes. But things are also good. And that good merits celebration leading to joy, joy like a steel spine, holding us upright.

My friend Brittany lost her husband four years ago. I've watched her grieve. Seen her devastation and also her unyielding hope. She wrote this on Facebook the other day: "My life has seen some high highs, but never a lower low than losing the man I was to spend forever with. Today marks four years since my world was forever changed by losing Bradford." She shared some of what she'd loved about Bradford, shared how lucky she felt to have been loved by him. But then she said how thankful she was for the new relationship in her life and the joys it brought. She said this joy didn't undo her pain but that instead she experienced both pain and joy. She wrote, "Joy has come, but grief remains."

> Joy has come, but grief remains.

There's power in opening ourselves up to joy—noticing the gifts around us, participating in celebration, seeking beauty and excellence. All of it goes against our grieving impulse to turn inward and close our eyes, to protect ourselves from further loss. But all of it, even the simplest acts like taking a walk in the sunshine or petting a passing dog or looking at pictures of a friend's new baby, every effort to see what's good is rewarded with an uptick in joy.

Ann Voskamp writes,

> When we lay the soil of our hard lives open to the rain of grace and let joy penetrate our cracked and dry places, let joy soak into our broken skin and deep crevices, life grows. How can this not be the best thing for the world? For us?[5]

I heard Kate Bowler say something similar in a podcast: "The pain digs something out, and the joy fills it."[6] In our grief, joy is the best thing for us, but to receive it we have to be willing to stand in the rain of grace, arms open, vulnerable to beauty and blessing.

When we lay the soil of our hard lives open to the rain of grace and let joy penetrate our cracked and dry places, let joy soak into our broken skin and deep crevices, life grows. How can this not be the best thing for the world? For us?

You might ask, what joy could be enough in a world without the person I love? Only the joy of the Lord. Hikes and parties and puppies are a start, but only if we see *through* them *to* God and only if in them we're pointed to greater, deeper sources of strength, sources like presence and comfort and hope. When we try to find joy in the blessings themselves and not in the Giver, when we voraciously seek pleasures, delights, adrenaline hits, and momentary thrills, we find ourselves disappointed. Like my husband's second sandwich, they're not enough. They never last. And sometimes they're not even truly good. What I've seen in my grief is that there's a gift in the toppling of tiny idols, in the forcible removal of the toothpick scaffolding that once held up my mood. Because of grief, I can no longer depend on temporary hits of happiness, a second chai tea latte or a third hour on the couch watching Netflix. I've had to see and seek something stronger, the joy of the Lord.

When we seek reasons for joy, combing through our God-given circumstances, we'll find it in God's promises—his promise of presence here on earth, his promise of transformation into the image of Christ, his promise to redeem evil for good, his promise of a guiding Spirit, his promise of eternal life, and his promise of community and belonging. We won't just find it in the promises, either. We'll also find joy in the fulfillment of those promises happening around us all the time.

Perhaps one of the most unexpected sources of joy is the one we mentioned from James, "Consider it pure joy, my brothers and sisters, whenever you face trials of many kinds" (v. 2). Why do we find joy in trials? Not because trials are good (they're not), but because trials accomplish something good. James says, "Because you know that the testing of your faith produces perseverance. Let perseverance finish its work so that you may be mature and complete, not lacking anything" (3–4). Your difficult circumstances have the potential to bless you, and in that blessing you can find joy.

If it feels like we've come full circle, we have.

Grief, though terrible, carries with it gifts, opportunities for growth and blessing, and when we embrace those gifts we find joy. Joy then is the reward of a grief received.

Celebrate

Since Bobby died I've grown quite adept at the discipline of joy and the practice of celebration. I've learned how to throw a killer party, one that glorifies God through story and spectacle. I've learned how to track and celebrate blessings, keeping journals, blogging,

> The loss of joy does not make the world better—and, conversely, refusing joy for the sake of suffering does not help those who suffer. The contrary is true. The world needs people who discover the good, who rejoice in it and thereby derive the impetus and courage to do good. Joy, then, does not break with solidarity. When it is the right kind of joy, when it is not egotistic, when it comes from the perception of the good, then it wants to communicate itself, and it gets passed on. In this connection, it always strikes me that in the poor neighborhoods of, say, South America, one sees many more laughing happy people than among us. Obviously, despite all their misery, they still have the perception of the good to which they cling and in which they can find encouragement and strength.
>
> —Pope Benedict XVI, when he was Joseph Cardinal Ratzinger, *Salt of the Earth: The Church at the End of the Millennium*[7]

texting. I've learned how to make a moment memorable so I don't forget the good that God's done; once I stopped my car on the side of the road and ran into the woods to pray in a way befitting my experience of God's glory. I've learned to build altars with my family (big and small reminders of God's presence and deliverance). In a real way, grief taught me how to have joy.

In a real way, grief taught me how to have joy.

Early on, my parents and Justin and I wanted some way to remember Bobby and celebrate his life. My parents settled on a scholarship in his name and an annual benefit dinner to raise money. Every year we planned a giant event with great food, entertainment, and an auction. Once Justin and a friend performed songs from early nineties sitcoms. People sang along to every word of the *Golden Girls* theme. One year we had a putting contest. Another year a game of high-stakes, buy-in knock out—the children's basketball game. We usually sang hymns together and prayed at the end. Always it was a grand reunion of people who'd loved Bobby and people Bobby loved.

The very first year we took a giant group photo. Just before the camera clicked someone yelled, "Pretend you're asleep! Like Bobby would have!" And we all pretended we'd fallen asleep, a common gag of Bobby's when you turned away from him and looked back. I look at that picture now, two hundred people, all of us grown adults, all of us grieving a friend, all of us pretending to sleep, and I see the power of joy to make grief lighter.

I see the power of joy to make grief lighter.

Every year we sold a different T-shirt to benefit the scholarship. About three years in, Justin texted me with a T-shirt idea. He said, "How about this: My friend Bobby went to heaven and all I got was this lousy T-shirt?" At lunch when I read it, I choked on my salad. Laughing, I showed it to everyone at my table and typed back, "That's perfect." After a few seconds my phone buzzed, and I looked down to see his text back. He wrote, "It's funny, but it's not true. Not at all."

For Reflection and Discussion

1 Do you feel robbed of joy in your grief? What used to bring you joy that doesn't anymore?

2 What have you tried to make yourself happy since your loved one died? Is it working?

3 What's bringing you joy right now? Make as long a list as you can.

4 Are you closing yourself off to joy? If so, how might you open yourself up? Where do you need to start looking?

5 What promises of God bring you joy in hope? List a few.

6 How might you intentionally practice celebration to grow in joy? Plan a get-together, gathering, or party.

Resources

Deraniyagala, Sonali. *Wave*.

Never in my life have I read anything as sad as the story in this book. A memoir of her own loss (Deraniyagala lost her husband and two sons in a tsunami), the days and weeks outlined here examine the lowest points of grief. This book, well written and gripping, reminds me that grief won't naturally lead to joy; it doesn't in this story, and it often doesn't in the lives of people we love.

Bowler, Kate. *Everything Happens* podcast.

In this podcast (a play on the oft-repeated platitude "everything happens for a reason") Bowler interviews wise and experienced sufferers to explore what can be learned in particularly dark times. See especially episodes 1 with Nadia Bolz-Weber and 3 with Dr. Lucy Kalanithi.

Notes

Chapter 1: Changing Shape

1. C. S. Lewis, *A Grief Observed* (London: Faber & Faber, 2012).
2. Revisionist History podcast, season 2, episode 5, "The Prime Minister and the Prof."
3. Katherine Mansfield, "The Canary," in *The Dove's Nest and Other Stories* (London: Constable, 1923), 60.
4. Charles Dickens, *Dombey and Son*, chapter 18: https://tinyurl.com/ybrduy4t.
5. Samuel J. Hodges and Kathy Leonard, *Grieving with Hope: Finding Comfort as You Journey through Loss* (Grand Rapids: Baker, 2011), 22.

Chapter 2: Fighting for Life

1. John W. James and Russell Friedman, *The Grief Recovery Handbook: The Action Program for Moving Beyond Death, Divorce, and Other Losses including Health, Career, and Faith*, 20th anniversary expanded edition (New York: HarperCollins, 2009), 31.
2. Anne Morrow Lindbergh, *Return to the Sea* (Philadelphia, PA: Innisfree, 1998), 97.
3. Melina Marchetta, *On the Jellicoe Road* (Melbourne, Australia: Penguin, 2006) e-book.
4. Charles Frazier, *Cold Mountain* (New York: Atlantic Monthly Press, 1997), 334.
5. Elizabeth Gilbert, *Eat, Pray, Love* (New York: Bloomsbury, 2016), 75.
6. Neil Gaiman, *Sandman: Fables and Reflections* (New York: Warner Books/DC Comics, 1994).

Chapter 3: Practicing Hope

1. Gabriel García Márquez, *No One Writes to the Colonel*, trans. J. S. Bernstein (London: Penguin, 1996), 43.

2. Haruki Murakami, *Kafka on the Shore*, trans. Philip Gabriel (New York: Vintage International, 2006), 6.
3. Philip Yancey, *Where Is God When It Hurts?* 7th ed. (New York: HarperCollins, 1990), 109.
4. Barbara Kingsolver, *Animal Dreams* (New York: HarperPerennial, 2013), 299.
5. John Green, *The Fault in Our Stars* (New York: Dutton Books, 2012), 286.

Chapter 4: Exploding Safely: The Gift of Lament

1. David Biro, *The Language of Pain: Finding Words, Compassion, and Relief* (New York: W.W. Norton, 2010), 11.
2. Peter Enns, "When God Is Unfaithful: Reclaiming a Theology of Lament," https://tinyurl.com/y7ho5cnr.
3. Esther Fleece, "5 Things You Need to Know about Lament," The Evangelical Pulpit, January 9, 2017, https://tinyurl.com/ya5lxqyk.

Chapter 5: Welcoming Help: The Gift of Belonging

1. Andrew Murray, "Humility," originally published in New York: Anson D. F. Randolph & Co., 1895, https://tinyurl.com/y8sxbe5h.
2. Joan Gould, "On the Graceful Art of Receiving Gifts," *New York Times*, December 25, 1981, https://tinyurl.com/y97dnufz.

Chapter 6: Living in the Present: The Gift of Daily Bread

1. Jerry L. Sittser, *A Grace Disguised: How the Soul Grows through Loss* (Grand Rapids: Zondervan, 2004), 147.
2. Andy Stanley, *Enemies of the Heart: Breaking Free from the Four Emotions That Control* (Colorado Springs: Multnomah, 2011), 57.
3. Alexander Maclaren, "Anxious Care," a sermon published in 1859, https://tinyurl.com/yadhhdfu.
4. C. S. Lewis, *The Weight of Glory: And Other Addresses* (New York: HarperOne, 2001), 61.

Chapter 7: Seeing Clearly: The Gifts of Mortality and Immortality

1. Joan Didion, *The Year of Magical Thinking* (New York: Alfred A. Knopf, 2005), 4.
2. Rob Bell, *Drops Like Stars* (Grand Rapids: Zondervan 2010), 27–30.

3. Seneca, "On the Shortness of Life." Full text here: https://tinyurl.com/y98kbuzj.
4. Rafael Yglesias, *A Happy Marriage* (New York: Scribner, 2010), 263.
5. Marcus Aurelius, *The Emperor's Handbook: A New Translation of The Meditations*, trans. C. Scot Hicks and David V. Hicks (New York: Scribner, 2002), meditations II.4, 28.

Chapter 8: Remembering: The Gift of Inspiration

1. Mitch Albom, *For One More Day* (New York: Hachette, 2008), **XX**.
2. Marcus Tullius Cicero, "The 14 Orations Against Marcus Antonius" (Oration 9, part V), trans. C. D. Yonge, 1903, https://tinyurl.com/yafe5yeo.
3. Bruce Feiler, "The Stories That Bind Us," *New York Times*, March 15, 2013.

Chapter 9: Reaching Out: The Gift of Comfort

1. C. S. Lewis, *The Four Loves* (New York: HarperOne, 2017), 100.
2. Rob Bell, *Drops Like Stars* (Grand Rapids: Zondervan, 2010), 65.
3. Bell, *Drops Like Stars*, 68.
4. Bell, *Drops Like Stars*, 68.

Chapter 10: Looking for Light: The Gift of Gratitude

1. *The Practical Works of Richard Baxter*, vol. 4 (London: George Virtue, Paternoster Row, 1838), 932.
2. Ann Voskamp, *One Thousand Gifts: A Dare to Live Fully Right Where You Are* (Grand Rapids: Zondervan, 2010), 58.
3. Robert Emmons, "Why Gratitude Is Good," *Greater Good Magazine*, November 16, 2010, https://tinyurl.com/ycwavsnb.
4. Emmons, "Why Gratitude Is Good."
5. Henry Ward Beecher, *Leadership* 7, no. 2.
6. Thornton Wilder, *The Woman of Andros* (New York: Albert & Charles Boni, 1930), 36
7. Melody Beattie, *Gratitude: Inspirations* (Center City, MN: Hazelden, 2007), 8.
8. Thomas Merton, *Thoughts in Solitude* (New York: Farrar, Straus & Giroux, 1958), 33.

Chapter 11: Rebuilding: The Gift of a New Normal

1. Granger E. Westberg, *Good Grief* (Minneapolis: Fortress Press, 2011), 89.
2. T. H. White, *The Once and Future King* (New York: Ace Books, 2011), 176.
3. Rabbi Joshua Liebman, *Peace of Mind* (New York: Carol Publishing Group, 1994), 114.

Chapter 12: Cultivating Joy: The Gift of Celebration

1. J. R. R. Tolkien, *The Silmarillion* (New York: Random House, 2002), 190.
2. Shelley Ramsey, *Grief: A Mama's Unwanted Journey* (Bloomington, IN: West Bow, 2013), 97.
3. Mary Oliver, "We Shake with Joy," in *Evidence: Poems by Mary Oliver* (Boston: Beacon, 2009), 13.
4. Barbara Kingsolver, *High Tide in Tucson: Essays from Now or Never* (New York: HarperPerennial, 2003), 15.
5. Ann Voskamp, *One Thousand Gifts: A Dare to Live Fully Right Where You Are* (Grand Rapids: Zondervan, 2010), 58.
6. Kate Bowler, "The Insight of Outsiders," February 6, 2018, in *Everything Happens*, produced by Duke University, podcast, https://katebowler.com/everything-happens/.
7. Joseph Cardinal Ratzinger, *Salt of the Earth: The Church at the End of the Millennium* (San Francisco: Ignatius Press, 1997), 36